Between
Silence and Speech

Dear AJ,

I thought you might appreciate this. Enjoy,

Y. F.

Between Silence and Speech

Essays on Jewish Thought

Nathan T. Lopes Cardozo

JASON ARONSON INC.
Northvale, New Jersey
London

The author gratefully acknowledges permission to reprint the following:

"Maimonides, Silence and the World of Sacrifices," by Nathan T. Lopes Cardozo, in *Le'ela* (April 1992): 32-35. Copyright © 1992 by Jews' College. Used by permission.

"Maimonides, Silence and the World of Sacrifices," by Nathan T. Lopes Cardozo, in *Living With Torah*, a series of Torah lectures (1992): 41-51. Copyright © 1992 by Jeff Seidel. Used by permission.

"Particularisme en Universalisme," by Nathan T. Lopes Cardozo, in Dr. G. H. Cohen Stuart, redactie, *Een bevrijdend woord uit Jeruzalem?* (1991): 67-78. Copyright © 1991 by Uitgeverij Boekencentrum B. V. Used by permission.

Selected excerpts from *To Have or to Be?* by Erich Fromm copyright © 1976 by Erich Fromm. Introduction copyright © 1976 by Ruth Nanda Anshen. Reprinted by permission of HarperCollins Publishers, Inc.

This book was set in 13 pt. Berkeley Oldstyle by Alpha Graphics of Pittsfield, New Hampshire, and printed by Book-mart Press in North Bergen, New Jersey.

Library of Congress Cataloging-in-Publication Data

Lopes Cardozo, Nathan T.
    Between silence and speech : essays on Jewish thought / Nathan T. Lopes Cardozo.
        p.   cm.
    Includes bibliographical references and index.
    ISBN 1-56821-336-0
    1. Judaism—20th century. 2. Judaism—Doctrines. 3. Jewish way of life. 4. Orthodox Judaism—Relations—Nontraditional Jews.
    I. Title.
    BM580.L576 1995
    296—dc20   94-37611

Manufactured in the United States of America. Jason Aronson Inc. offers books and cassettes. For information and catalog write to Jason Aronson Inc., 230 Livingston Street, Northvale, New Jersey 07647.

To my mother-in-law,
Rosa Gnesin Herskovits,
on the occasion of her eightieth birthday,
15 *Adar* 5754–Shushan Purim, 11 March 1994.

In memory of my father-in-law,
Grisha Gnesin *z"l*,
who left this world on 30 *Kislev* 5734.

Thanks to my dear friends Aron and Bep Spijer, The Hague,
Netherlands, for their kind generosity.

N.T.L.C.

A people profoundly religious,
a people whose very history has
been the history of an idea,
are to be made to feel again the truth,
that life of the spirit is not a thing apart,
that it is in every thought,
and every word and every act.

The submergence of self in the pursuit of an ideal,
the readiness to spend oneself without measure,
prodigally, almost ecstatically,
for something intuitively apprehended
as great and noble,
spend oneself one knows not why—
some of us like to believe that
this is what religion means.

Benjamin Nathan Cardozo
Justice of the Supreme Court
of the United States
1870-1938
Values, 1931

Contents

Preface

t has often been said that traditional Judaism is no longer a viable option for the intelligent Jew in the twentieth century. Many tell us that it has had its day and has to make room for philosophies that reflect what people today call "modernity." This often-repeated term leaves it up to each one of us to decide what we mean.

There is a remarkable similarity between many secularists and those who claim to be religious. Both take their own belief systems for granted. They are imprisoned within their own worldviews and are afraid of looking beyond. The claim of "fundamentalism" that is often used against the religious community exists as much, if not more so, in the secular community, which claims to be open-minded. Most secular Jews overlook many profound challenges to their own beliefs and are generally totally ignorant of even the most important foundations of Judaism or philosophical inquiry. They are, however, quick to state their opinions about the Jewish tradition.

The religious community, on the other hand, is often not prepared to consider a critical assessment of its beliefs and is, therefore, not able to understand the deeper intent behind much of the ideology of Judaism. In that way, it becomes a bad advocate of the sorely needed voice for authentic Judaism in our own days.

Over many years I have had the great privilege and pleasure to teach nonreligious people about Judaism—people of all ages and backgrounds, including professors, doctors, lawyers, university students, and businesspersons. Through my discussions with them I had an opportunity to learn much about their insights into life, their criticisms, and their urge to understand what it means to be a Jew. I soon recognized what lay at the bottom of these criticisms, since they expressed many of my skeptical thoughts concerning Judaism in my younger, "stubborn" years.

This experience enabled me to teach the Jewish tradition in a way that would challenge them, making them see its profundity and, above all, its relevance to modern man. My non-Jewish audiences have often told me that I helped them appreciate the message of Judaism for all men of the twentieth century.

These lectures should, therefore, be seen as a response to both the secular claim that Judaism no longer speaks to modern man and to many religious people who make the mistake of taking religious beliefs for granted.

I decided to write about some of those topics that disturbed me the most at a time, in my rebellious days, when I sincerely doubted the value of Judaism. Calling ourselves the Chosen People sounded to me like real *chutzpah* (audacity) and most dangerous. Moreover, in the case of the *mamzer* law, the injustice of making a child responsible for the misdeeds of his or her parents was, I believed, altogether intolerable and outrageous.

Maimonides' declaration that the sacrificial cult in the Temple is rooted in idolatry was more than shocking and put the authenticity of traditional Judaism into question for me. The halachic obsession with external deeds completely contradicted my understanding of genuine religion. Orthodox Judaism's uncompromising refusal to accept the findings of modern biblical scholarship looked more than pretentious. The redundant prayer-liturgy became another example of how much Judaism was out of touch with the needs of spiritual man. *Shabbat* observance, with all its restrictions, was a relic from the past, and the prohibition of mixing milk and meat, an anachronism reflecting primitive laws of a misguided hygienic code.

However, when I began to study Judaism more carefully, I was forced to admit that I had been badly mistaken and that my "skepticism" was based on ignorance and a complete misreading of Judaism's prerogatives. To my utter amazement, it started to dawn on me that the very issues I had mocked were perhaps the most profound expressions of Judaism's wisdom. This journey of discovery was, however, far from easy. It was a struggle, and it took a long time before I was able to make some peace with my newly found discoveries.

Once I realized what had happened, I felt obligated to inform my students of my discoveries, and now, many years later, I have decided to make some of these lectures available to a reading audience. This does not mean that the topics no longer bother me or that there is no longer a place for hard questions and debate, but I have learned to respect the Jewish tradition for its honesty and its ongoing struggle to understand the word of God. Additionally, I have added a few other lectures that are more theoretical in nature but show something of the originality and profundity of the Jewish tradition.

I am not sure if there is really anything new in what I have to say. Thousands of original thinkers have had their hand in Judaism over the last three thousand years. As such, it is nearly impossible to claim originality. In such a rich tradition one may even believe that one is being original without being aware of having been preceded by someone else. Nonetheless, I have tried to present some of my own ideas— and, I hope, with some success.

At this moment in time, the State of Israel is experiencing one of its greatest challenges. It is trying to make peace with an organization that for many years has tried to destroy its very foundations. To achieve this goal, the Jewish State is taking enormous risks, which most world nations do not appreciate. Many Israelis have become confused and insecure. While it is unclear how the peace agreement will affect the future of this little state, one thing is clear—all of world Jewry is holding its breath. Israel's very existence is at stake. Only a strong feeling of solidarity, a deep commitment toward a common goal, and a feeling of mission will keep Jews and Israelis from despair.

Throughout all of its short history, the Israeli State has suffered from a lack of identity. From its very inception, it has struggled with its Jewish makeup and lacked the strength to inspire its citizens to face the full meaning of their Jewishness. I believe that this is Israel's greatest dilemma. Only when the nation's leaders and educators realize that Jews are Jews because of their tradition and unique way of life will there be good reason to believe that the state will rise above all its predicaments. The driving force behind a nation is its spiritual purpose combined with an unremitting will to turn this purpose into its pride and destination. When Jews realize this and understand that Judaism's message is today more relevant than ever, they will once more find the inner tranquillity for which they long so intensely.

I hope that the essays in this book will contribute to this goal.

Acknowledgments

ost of the essays in this book were delivered as lectures to audiences in many countries. Some of them were given at Israeli colleges in which I have taught Jewish Philosophy and Ideology. Others were given at university campuses such as the Hebrew University in Jerusalem and Wits University in Johannesburg, South Africa. Still others were addressed to the Jewish Student Organizations of the universities of Oxford and Cambridge in England. Some lectures were also delivered at theological conferences and institutes of non-Jewish institutions.

I am thankful to Rabbi Dr. David Refson, dean of Neve Yerushalaim College for Jewish Studies; Rabbi Dr. Yehudah Copperman, Dean of Michlala Jerusalem College for Women; and Rabbi Dr. Shalom Gold of the Jerusalem College for Adults for giving me the opportunity to deliver some of these lectures in their colleges.

Since my views on Judaism are not always in agreement with those of the ultra-Orthodox, or as thought by some of my dear colleagues in Yeshivath Ohr Somayach, I greatly appreciate its dean, Rabbi Dr. Nota Schiller, for giving me the opportunity to expose its students to different views within traditional Judaism. This shows courage and intellectual integrity.

Above all, I am thankful to my students, who often challenged some of the ideas expressed in these lectures. This has helped me tremendously in restructuring the lectures and adding what was lacking.

Some of these essays have appeared in journals or books. "On Silence and Sacrifices" appeared in the English rabbinical journal Le'ela (Jews' College Publications) and in "Living with Torah," sponsored by the Jewish Information Center in Jerusalem in December 1992. "On Particularism and Universalism" was first published in a Dutch book titled, *Een bevrijdend woord uit Jeruzalem?*, a collection of essays edited by my friend Dr. G. H. Cohen Stuart (Boekencentrum B.V., 1991). "On the Primordial Torah" was privately published for my students by Bep Ron Publications in 1988.

I thank Mike Kramer and an anonymous friend of mine for helping me finance the editing of these essays, and I also thank Rabbi Yechiel Krohner for organizing, for some years now, many of my lecture tours in the United States and, in so doing, for stimulating me to create new lectures to be delivered in the United States and Canada. Special mention should also be made of the dedicated staff of the Introductory Program of Ohr Somayach headed by rabbis Michael Schoen and Reuven Geffen, who make it a pleasure to teach in that school. I thank Rabbi Yehoshua Karsch for reading and commenting on some of the essays.

All the essays were edited by my gifted student Nati Gamedze, whose unique sense for languages has made him into an academic expert. His careful reading of the complete manuscript and his improvements greatly increased the read-

ability of this book. Another student of mine, Laurence Little-
stone, wrote a few of the articles based on earlier manuscripts.
His beautiful English stands out. Mrs. Els Bendheim and Rabbis Yehoshua Levine and Shlomo Fox-Ashrei gave numerous
suggestions for improving the style and content of chapter 7.

I had the great merit to study for many years in Gateshead Yeshiva in England, Europe's most illustrious institute
for Jewish studies. To its great teachers I am most grateful
for their permission to enter their institution at a time when
I could not even read proper Hebrew and lacked all basic
talmudic knowledge. Looking back to those days, I realize
that I must have been quite a nuisance, asking most unusual
questions (to say the least) and making unconventional observations. Nonetheless, all of the lecturers showed endless patience and even provided me with private classes. No words
can express the gratitude I owe them.

Over many years I have had the opportunity to read far
beyond what the average *yeshivah* education encompasses. I
have taken note of modern Jewish thought and of philosophical thought in general. I have debated Judaism with some
apikorsim (heretics), and tried to understand the secular
mind. All this has greatly helped me to understand my students, showing me new ways of teaching Judaism. Above all,
it convinced me that traditional Judaism carries a most ar-
ticulate message for man and has all the power to overcome
the criticism of secular ideologies.

This book is dedicated to my mother-in-law, a remarkable lady who has become one of my best friends since I
married her daughter more than twenty-five years ago. We
have shared many jokes together and lately derive a lot of
nachat (no English translation possible) from her great-grand-
children who happen, by divine intervention, to be my grandchildren—"*Ad mea ve-esrim!*"

My father-in-law of blessed memory, who was born in the town of Sklov, was a most unusual Jew. Mentally, he continued to live in this East European metropolis of Jewish learning even after he resettled in the small Dutch town of Haarlem. In his latter years he suffered greatly but never faltered in his commitment to Judaism.

My dear mother, may she live many more years, is another unusual person who made it possible for me to live a full, religious Jewish life starting at the age of sixteen and did everything to help me succeed. Her incredible courage in the time of the Holocaust saved most of my father's family.

My dear father of blessed memory, who introduced me into the world of philosophy, died in 5737 (1977). He was a proud member of the Spanish Portuguese Synagogue of Amsterdam. Throughout my youth he instilled in me much *gravidade*, a distinctive kind of life-style typical of the Spanish-Portuguese Jewish community of Amsterdam, which settled in the Netherlands in the seventeenth century. His spiritual and financial support allowed me to pursue my studies and gave me the courage to reach my goals. I miss him deeply.

I have to thank Chazan Abraham Lopes Cardozo of the Spanish-Portuguese Synagogue in New York and *le-havdil ben chaim le-chaim* Cantor Jossel Rosenblatt for accompanying me with their beautiful (recorded) *chazanut* while I sat in my study writing this book. Together with Mozart, Beethoven, Leonard Bernstein, and many others, they inspired me and put me into the right mood, as well as stimulated new ideas in my mind. Without music, no book can be written. In fact, writing is making music with words rather than notes.

My very dear friends Aron and Bep Spijer from Holland encouraged me to write this book. Not only did they tell me to start putting my thoughts onto paper but they also gave me the material support to do so. Their constant interest in my family and myself, together with their important advice, have become vital to all that I do. No words can express my gratitude to them. May they live a full and healthy life.

Special thanks go to our good friend Channa Shapiro, who made many suggestions that I incorporated in this book. Through writing *Between Silence and Speech* I also found a new friend: Arthur Kurzweil, vice president of Jason Aronson Inc., who offered me the opportunity to publish this book through his distinguished publishing house. It was my friend Michael Pomeranz of Jerusalem who made this *shidduch*. To both of them: Chazak baruch!

My married daughters, Debora Sara and Michal Avigail, supported by their husbands, Michael Cohen and Yitzchak Elchanan Walkin, and their children, have given me much *nachat*. Together with my son, Shimon Moshe Chezkiyahu, his dear wife, Chana Naomi, and their baby girl, they are a constant source of inspiration and support.

Above all, I thank my dear wife, Frijda Rachel, and our two younger daughters, Nechama Shulamith and Elisheva Yehudith, who have had the patience to live with me and keep on serving me coffee, tea, and other niceties until late into the night. Their constant love, encouragement, concern, and help are unparalleled.

May God bless all those mentioned above, together with all the members of the House of Israel and all those members of the nations of the world who long for real *shalom*.

1

On Silence, Sacrifices, and the Golden Calf

aimonides' thesis concerning the sacrificial cult sparked off one of the most interesting controversies in Jewish history. It would seem at first sight that he was more than a little embarrassed by the sacrificial service in the Temple. The killing of animals, the spilling of the blood, the burning of the kidneys, limbs, and so on—in short, the gore and rituals related to the sacrifices—would appear to be difficult to accept as a representation of the highest ideals of monotheism and Jewish values.

It could therefore be argued that Maimonides found himself in a most awkward position. On the one hand, the sacrificial cult could not be seen as the pinnacle of Jewish ethics and humanitarianism. On the other, it could not be excluded from Jewish tradition since it is part and parcel of the divine text of the Torah.

Maimonides' attempt to synthesize these two seemingly irreconcilable positions, to simultaneously include and exclude this expression of Jewish ritual, is a masterpiece in ingenuity. The sacrificial cult had to be seen as a concession to human weakness. It had to be seen as a process of weaning the people away from idol worship, until a time when the ideal situation would prevail, when it would no longer be necessary. Viewed from this perspective, it did not have to represent Judaism par excellence and it could still be within the boundaries of Jewish tradition.

> It is impossible to go suddenly from one extreme to the other; the nature of man will not allow him suddenly to discontinue everything to which he has been accustomed. Now God sent Moses to make the Israelites a kingdom of priests and a holy nation. . . .
>
> The Israelites were commanded to devote themselves to His service. But the general mode of worship in which the Israelites were brought up (in earlier days) consisted of sacrificing animals in temples containing images, bowing down to these images, and burning incense before them.
>
> It was in accordance with the wisdom of God, as displayed in the whole creation, that He did not command us to give up and discontinue all these modes of worship, for to obey such a commandment would have been contrary to the nature of man.
>
> For this reason God allowed these rituals to continue. He transferred to His service that which had formerly served as a worship of created beings . . . and commanded us to serve Him in the same manner.[1]

But this explanation raises almost more questions than it solves. Did Maimonides really believe that this is all there was to temple sacrifices? Was there no deeper meaning, no greater symbolism? He seems to suggest that the sacrificial cult started within the world of idol worship, only later to become part of Judaism. Was not the first recorded incident of sacrificial offering that of Kain and Hevel (Cain and Abel) who, without doubt, brought their sacrifices to God and to no other entity (Genesis, chap. 4)? There is a strong internal contradiction within Maimonides' own works. While here he seems to suggest that ultimately, mankind (and the Jewish People) will attain a more exalted spiritual plane and, therefore, no longer be in need of bringing sacrifices, in his *Mishneh Torah* he seems to hold a different position: "The *Melech Mashiach* [Messiah] will arise in the future and restore the Kingship of the House of David, reestablishing its sovereignty; he will rebuild the Sanctuary and gather in all the dispersed of Israel. In his days all the laws will regain their validity; *sacrifices will again be offered.*"[2]

Thus, the question remains in even starker contrast. Will there be sacrifices in the Messianic Age as an expression of an exalted spiritual existence, or will there be no need for sacrifices since they are nothing more than a concession to human weakness?

In their prayers, Jews recite thrice daily: "Lord, O God, look with favor on Your People . . . speedily restore worship in Your Temple . . . and accept favorably and with love, Israel's sacrifices."[3] So how did Maimonides reconcile this with his observation in the *Guide*? Finally, is he suggesting, if only by implication, that a good part of the Book of Leviticus (which discusses most of the sacrificial laws) and the other books of Torah (Five Books of Moses) do not convey authentic Jewish ideology?

In the *Guide*, after the above-quoted words, Maimonides continues with another highly unusual remark:

If God were to ordain the elimination of the sacrifices, this would be as if a prophet were to come, in our time, who called to the service of God by saying: "The Lord has commanded you that you do not pray to Him, and that you do not fast, and that you do not implore His help in time of trouble, but rather that your service [of Him] consist [only] of thought without action."[4]

Adding perplexity upon perplexity, one may legitimately exclaim: What exactly is Maimonides trying to say? Is he saying that prayer and fasting must also be seen as concessions to human weakness? More markedly, is he perhaps suggesting that other *mitzvot* are also somehow a concession, since he gives prayer and fasting only as examples? The ultimate form of worship is, after all, contemplation, without worship or action.

THE TENT OF MEETING

In order to resolve these problems and paradoxes one must examine the temporal center of worship and prayer—the Temple itself. The very nature of this place of worship is rooted in the existence of an earlier place of religious elevation: the Tent of Meeting, a sort of movable Temple.

On the verse "And you shall make it" (Exodus 25:9), relating to the construction of the Tent of Meeting, the famous Italian commentator Ovadia Sforno (sixteenth century) made the following remarkable statement:

> In order that I shall dwell between you, to speak with you and to accept the prayers and the service of Israel. *This is not as it was before the sin of the Golden Calf, where it was said: "In any place where I shall have My name mentioned, I shall come to you and bless you."*[5] (italics added)

And a little later:

For at the end of the first forty days God gave the tablets made by Himself to sanctify all as priests and a Holy nation, as He had promised. *But they rebelled and became corrupt, and fell from this high spiritual level.*[6] (italics added)

The Tent of Meeting (and therefore the Temple), says Sforno, are the result of Israel's choice to do evil—to opt for the Golden Calf. In other words, had the Golden Calf incident never taken place, the directive to build a Tent of Meeting would never have been given.

What becomes exceedingly clear is that the *real* Temple, as the site of divine service, is not limited to the finite world. Its rightful place is the whole universe and that which is beyond the universe: "In *any* place where I shall have My Name mentioned I shall come to you." Clearly, God's greatness is beyond all physical limitations and encompasses the universe and the "worlds" beyond the universe.

If this is the thrust of God's original intention, then what is the need for a physical place to symbolize God's dwelling in this world? What purpose is served by the many ritual objects like the Altar, the *Menorah,* and the Ark in the Holy of Holies? Sforno suggests that the need for these "props" is the direct outcome of the sin of the Golden Calf.

THE SIN OF THE GOLDEN CALF

What was the essence of this sin? What mental construct was reflected in this transgression, in which so many of the Jews were involved?

The sin itself could obviously not have been a regular

form of idol worship: Only a short while earlier, the Jewish People had experienced a divine revelation of unprecedented intensity. The spoken word of God reached them in an open encounter and was of unquestionable veracity. In one voice the entire people avowed their commitment—"*Na'aseh ve-Nishma.*" "We shall do and we shall hear" (Exodus 24:7). Once and for all, the existence of God and His relationship to this world had been established. And still the question cries out to be answered—after all this, how could the sin of the Golden Calf have come about? We must conclude that the creation of the Golden Calf has to be seen as an attempt to deal with this overwhelming experience. After all, to deal with an experience like this requires vast spiritual resources. It demands a spiritual level of unprecedented heights, and above all, the abolition of any physical symbol of the Divinity. In short, this is monotheism, which is the realization of the unitary and unique nature of God in its most advanced form. *And even that which flows forth from God's unity cannot fully be captured in the mundane.* In its ideal state, Judaism should have had no need for symbolism altogether. Man would only be permitted to *contemplate* matters of the monotheistic world.

This, however, was unattainable for the generation of the Exodus, which only shortly before had been steeped in a world of idol worship. To hold on to the unprecedented Sinai experience was only possible, so they believed, through a tangible and, therefore, more down-to-earth medium— otherwise it was in danger of slipping away, dissipating into a spiritual nothingness with no real implication, nor indeed eternal validity.

This is undoubtedly the leitmotiv behind the episode of the Golden Calf. There was a perceived need to create guarantees ensuring the establishment of the revelatory experience of Sinai as an ongoing experience. The form of a calf, symbolic of the godhead in the cultural milieu of Egypt, from which the people had so recently emerged (and also, later, seen by kabbalistic tradition as a symbol of immense spiritual power), was understood to be the most appropriate way to accomplish this goal. It was, however, clear to all involved that this was not meant to be, nor was it perceived as, the monotheistic godhead *itself*. It was merely a symbol of the Creator and Mover of the Universe in mundane terms.

This, then, was the reason behind the fashioning of the Golden Calf. However, the creation of this image brought into being a completely different situation. Sforno's level of monotheism was not yet within the reach of the Israelite people. The fashioning of the Golden Calf showed that the people still could not relate to God without resorting to symbolism. The symbol-*less* world of ultimate monotheism had, perforce, to accede to a symbol-*full* monotheism.

The use of symbolic representation is, however, not without its dangers. This is exactly what the incident of the Golden Calf demonstrates. Because of their great, emotive power in the world of human imagination, symbols can easily lead to a spiritual misunderstanding. Wrong conclusions may be drawn from a misplaced symbol. It is often beyond man's capabilities to create appropriate representations himself. Man may never grasp the metaphysical world to such an extent that he can reflect it within the mundane. Therefore, symbols of this kind *can* only be *received*. They cannot be deduced by the limited mind of man.

What the makers of the Golden Calf did not understand was that no symbol could ever encompass the essence of God Himself. Even when a symbol might otherwise be called for, only God's way of *dealing in and with* this world may be reflected in a symbol—*not* His essence. Only God Himself can adequately conjure up and command an appropriate, yet still approximate, symbol.

Hence, the divine command for the Tent of Meeting was a more human, more mundane, and therefore more symbolic way of getting across the great values of monotheism, while still reminding us, however, of its ultimate symbol-*less* monotheism. As suggested by Sforno, the call for the Tent of Meeting can only be seen as a *concession to human weakness*.

THE IMPUDENCE OF PRAYER

The prayer book instructs the *chazan* (communual reader) to open the main body of prayers with: "*Barchu et Ha-Shem Ha-Mevorach*" (Praise You the Lord, Who is ultimately praised). The congregation, however, is requested to *simultaneously* say: "His name is *elevated above* all praises and blessings." This is intoned in silence, after which the community responds in a loud voice with: "*Baruch Ha-Shem Ha-Mevorach le-olam va-ed*" (Praised is the Lord, who is ultimately praised). This is, to say the least, something of a paradox: First there is a call to praise God, which is simultaneously belied by a statement that His name is *elevated beyond* all praises and blessings. In other words, praising God is an impossibility— it is beyond man's capabilities! After this, the community continues to praise God, as if to say that it *is* within the power of man to praise God after all.

The same paradox may be found in the *Kaddish* prayer: "May [God's] great Name be exalted and hallowed in the world of His creation. . . . He is . . . honored, exalted, glorified, adored [etc.]." Suddenly, the worshiper is asked to radically change direction: "[God] is *beyond* the power of all blessings, hymns, praise, and consolation that are said in this world and now say: Amen."

This paradox is reflected in a unique story related in the Talmud: Rabbi Chanina once observed a worshiper in the act of praising God with numerous additional laudations: not only was God "great," "mighty," and "powerful" but also "majestic," "awesome," "strong," "fearless," "sure," honored," and so forth.[7] Rabbi Chanina waited for the worshiper to conclude and then asked him if he really thought he had praised God sufficiently! The Talmud tells us that one should only praise God by the three words that Moshe used and leave it at that. Man may begin praising God, but he can never do so sufficiently; therefore, any attempt only succeeds in *limiting*, however fulsome it may be. The more praises one heaps on, the more one ultimately confines God's attributes. This is nothing short of blasphemy.

The message of this story is that in reality, man should be speechless before God. To grasp the greatness of God should render him silent. No words can ever suffice to extol the awesomeness of this experience. Silence is therefore the highest expression of prayer.

So why do we not stand in a prayer of silent contemplation? Why utter words if no words can ever suffice? The answer is now clear to us: the "prayer of words" is (once more) a concession to human weakness. Man, because of his weakness, cannot stand in contemplative silence; even in *meaningful* silence he cannot grasp the immense greatness of God. His mind cannot grasp what his heart knows.

In the midst of such a silence, his mind would wander, and paradoxically, the focus of his attention would shift away from his Creator. In this state of human weakness, man starts to look for other ways to concentrate his mind on his Maker. This, then, is the function of the verbal prayer. It is more down-to-earth, more tangible, and therefore, more appropriate to man's condition. Such is the secret of prayer.

This is precisely what Maimonides meant. Man's real

and full *confrontation* with God can only be conducted in silent, actionless contemplation. The overpowering experience of real prayer would leave him in a state of such deep humility that nothing could adequately be done or said. *Anything less than that is basically a concession.*

Maimonides' understanding of Judaism, therefore, is one in which concession to human weakness is not only essential, but also absolute. All *mitzvot* are essentially concessions, since the experience of God in a most advanced form cannot lead to anything other than contemplation and inaction.

THE FUTURE OF SACRIFICES

We may now return to our original discussion regarding Maimonides' attitude toward the sacrificial cult. Even for Maimonides, sacrifices have a deep religious meaning, albeit a symbolic one.[8] What he is telling us, however, is that there are different stages in the way in which the Jews will, in the future, relate to the sacrificial cult.

In the first stage of the Messianic Era, the Jew will again be required to bring sacrifices: Within the world of concession, *the world in which Halachah operates*, the sacrifices will once more become essential to Jewish worship. This is clearly portrayed in Maimonides' halachic masterpiece, *Mishneh Torah*. But in the *Guide*, in which he lays down his *metaphysical* system, Maimonides looks beyond the world of concession. Here, he discusses his conception of supreme monotheism, in which only contemplation is the most eloquent expression of man's deepest religious motivation.

Within Judaism, the sacrificial cult of *korbanot*, the deepest expression of man's close relationship with God, is nonetheless no more than a *symbol*, representing through form and action that absolute proximity. Ultimately, this *mitzvah*, like all other *mitzvot*, will find expression in the purest form of drawing close to God in monotheistic worship: contemplation.

The Temple as the site of interaction with the divine can, as suggested by Sforno, reflect nothing less than the entire universe and beyond. By definition, the physical is incapable of holding the metaphysical. This is, no doubt, the meaning behind the statement of the Sages that the Third Temple will, in a later stage of the Messianic Age, be transformed into a "Temple of fire."[9]

IDOL WORSHIP

Regarding Maimonides' observation that the sacrificial cult started in the world of *avodah zarah* (idol worship), we may suggest that he did not wish to imply that sacrifices were first brought by idol worshipers. This would contradict the very story of Kain and Hevel (Cain and Abel). What he had in mind (and this is borne out by a close study of the text) was to convey the message that the sacrificial cult started in *avodah zarah* (literally, *strange* worship). It is strange and alien because it did not represent *ultimate* monotheism as conceived by Sforno. Supreme monotheism, being the realization of divine unity, can only allow for *korbanot* (sacrifices) in a *contemplative* sense—only in the mind of men. The story of Kain and Hevel occurred *after* the Fall and therefore could no longer represent this lofty ideal.

Only before the Fall in the Garden of Eden was there the paradigm of pure monotheism: contemplation and inaction resulting from the overpowering experience of the divine.

SINAI

We may posit that the above-mentioned "theology of silence" is already alluded to in Exodus (20:15). There we read how at the overwhelming Sinai experience, the people "saw the sounds and the flames and the tones of the *shofar*," after which "the people trembled and stood afar." On this, Rashi remarks: "They *saw* that which is normally impossible to see" (italics added).

R' Chaim Volozhin, in his *Nefesh Ha-Chaim*, remarks:[10]

> They heard what usually is seen, and they saw what was normally heard, that is to say: The material senses were so vitiated, and this perception so refined that all material things previously appreciated through the senses of sight could no longer be perceived as physical objects.

That which is of the highest spiritual form cannot be limited by description or grasped by man's five senses. Something which is essentially a spiritual entity cannot be described or envisaged. The metamorphosis of Sinai silenced the normal faculties of perception. Only the *essence* of things could be contemplated.

It is this that lies at the root of Maimonides' conception of supreme monotheism as reflected in the *Guide*, and that ultimately resolves the paradoxes that previously defied resolution. The experience of *Matan Torah* (the Revelation at Mount Sinai) restored man's potential to reach heights of spiritual awareness and development (which he consequently violated with the incident of the Golden Calf). Our task, says Maimonides, is to recognize and strive towards the realization of that potential.

2

On Sleep as Awareness

hy do human beings have to sleep? A good part of man's lifetime is spent in suspension, without any productivity or contribution to society.

In *Bereshit Rabbah* 8:10, we find a most illuminating observation:

When the Holy One Blessed be He, created Man, the Ministering Angels mistook Adam for a divine being and wished to exclaim "Holy" before him. What does this resemble? A king and a governor were riding together in a chariot. The king's subjects wished to greet their king with cries of "Sovereign," but they did not know which one was the king. What, then, did the king do? He pushed the governor out of the chariot and thereby the subjects knew who the king was. Similarly said Rabbi Hoshya, when God created Adam the angels mistook him [for God]. What, then, did the Holy One blessed be He do? He caused sleep to fall upon him, and thereby all knew he was a human being!

Why, one should ask, would the angels ever believe man to be a holy being, a divinity? Is the distinction between God and man not crystal clear?

13

Sleep also occurs in another context: *Shabbat*. The Jew is asked to sleep and rest on *Shabbat* and to refrain from work. On the other hand, *Shabbat* is definitely not just a day of idleness and leisure. Prayer and study sessions are called for. Sometimes, these require long walks to the synagogue or the community centers. Intensive and exhausting lectures may make the participants more than just a little tired. And many a man may be more than pleased to find his bed at the end of this holy day! This, however, goes hand in hand with many restrictions, such as abstaining from lighting a fire or an electric light, the comfort of driving a car, writing, or even carrying a small light object in the *reshut ha-rabim* (public domain). Not one of them is as trying as walking long distances or rising early to go to the synagogue for *Shabbat* prayers!

THE TENT OF MEETING
AND OVERRIDING THE *SHABBAT*

Regarding *Shabbat*: Why is it that the Book of Exodus records the command by God to observe the institution of *Shabbat* immediately *before* He instructs Moshe to build the Tent of Meeting?

> Moshe then convoked the whole Israelite community and said to them: These are the things the Lord has commanded you to do. On six days work should be done, but on the seventh day you shall have a Sabbath of complete rest, holy to the Lord; whoever does any work on it shall be put to death. You shall kindle no fire throughout your settlements on the Sabbath day. Moshe said further to the whole community of Israelites: This is what the Lord has commanded.

> . . . Let all among you who are skilled come and make all
> that the Lord has commanded: the Tabernacle, its tent and
> its covering, its caps and its planks, its bars. (35:1-11)

This, one could argue, is most surprising and repetitious.
On a much earlier occasion, the Torah informed us that the
Ten Commandments instructed the Jews to observe *Shabbat*:
"Remember the Sabbath day to keep it holy" (Exodus 20:8).
Why was there a repetition of this command just be-
fore the construction of the Tent of Meeting? Rashi (35:2),
recognizing the difficulty, states: "The Torah warns concern-
ing the command to observe the Sabbath before the one to
build the Tent, to tell you that the building of the Tent of
Meeting does not override the Law of Sabbath [observance]."
And elsewhere (31:12): "Although I [God] have told you to
be zealous and diligent concerning this work [of the Tent of
Meeting] one does not put aside the Sabbath for it."
This is indeed very surprising: Why should the observance of *Shabbat* be more important than building the Tent
of Meeting? Is not the Tent of Meeting more important than
Shabbat? After all, is not the Tent of Meeting the symbol of
the possibility of an *ongoing* encounter between God and
man, the greatest message Judaism carries? Only after the fact
is established that God "dwells" in the midst of man does it
make sense to observe the Sabbath. *Shabbat* is, after all, the
day on which one is asked to contemplate and recognize
afresh this very fact. Why keep *Shabbat* when God is not yet
"living among us"? One may even add that by making
Moshe's "men of skill" refrain from work on *Shabbat* one is,
in fact, postponing the moment when God's presence will
be represented in the world!
Abravanel, in his (fifteenth-century) work *Perush al Ha
Torah* (Exodus 35:1) alludes to this:

Since the Tent of Meeting and its vessels whose making God had commanded symbolize communion with Him and the resting of His presence on the nation, we might have thought that this activity outweighed in importance all the other biblical prescriptions and most certainly the Shabbath rest. . . . Actual work is a more eloquent witness of faith than cessation from work, since action is affirmation and inaction, negation. . . . It might well have been argued that the work of the Tent of Meeting would have sufficed to draw attention and testimony to the existence of the Divine Presence in our midst to His omnipotence as Creator of the world and all the creatures therein. The desistence from work would therefore not be required in this instance, to testify to these principles.

Abravanel, however, does not provide any answer to the puzzle.

FIRE

Two stories, one Jewish and the other one Greek, show the great difference in the weltanschauung between the Jew and the Greek. Both asked which medium is responsible for the progress and development of the world and both answered: fire. The creation of heat has made it possible for man to be able to build, advance scientific technology, and create comfort and different forms of enjoyment. Without fire the world would still be in its primordial form and would probably decompose. Fire is the primary force behind all human-made development.

The Greeks wondered how fire ever came to man. They understood that those who possess fire possess the world! So how did fire fall into the hands of man? The Greeks came to the conclusion that this fire must have been *stolen* for it to have fallen into the hands of men. The gods, the ultimate rulers, could never have consented willingly to men becoming the owners of fire. This would, after all, paralyze the very power of these gods. It was Prometheus, the brother of the god Zeus, who stole the fire of the gods—a crime for which he was consequently severely punished.

In contradistinction to this stands the Midrash of our Sages, which relates how God approached and pleaded with Adam to learn the skill of making fire. On Saturday night after the celebration of the first *Shabbat*, God brings two stones to Adam and teaches him how to make fire with them and how to use it. Adam, realizing the meaning of this gift, bursts out in a spontaneous *brachah* (blessing): "Blessed is He who has created the light of fire."[1] This, as we shall later explain, became the *brachah* that the Jew utters every Saturday night, just after the Sabbath has ended and before he reassumes his work as a creator.

According to the conceptual standards of Greek mythology, the gods were not willing to let the secret of the Creation out of their hands. Man is, therefore, bound by the powers of the gods and is nothing but a puppet in their hands. There is no cooperation or partnership.

Judaism stands in complete opposition to this philosophy: Man is created in the image of God. This means, amongst other things, that man is blessed with creativity and intellectual comprehension:

The characteristic endowment of a mentally normal human being is his intelligence. When the Torah says: Let us make Man in Our image, it refers to the human capacity to know and appreciate abstract conceptions, apart from particular physical objects.[2]

The task of man is "to fill the earth, master it and rule the fish of the sea" (Genesis 1:28). "This is a divine mandate for Man to harness the world, control and master nature in the fullest possible manner."[3]

The creative impetus is a divine gift. The active expression of human creativity is a divine injunction. The Creation has a normative message: it is a call for human action, for involvement and partnership with the Creator. The world was created in a dynamic state. With the creation of the world in the first six days, it was far from being a perfect place: it was uncultivated and still in an undeveloped and primitive form. But it held all the ingredients, all the potential to become a perfect and wonderful world. God's call to man is to continue what He started:

> All that was created in the six days, requires cultivation, like mustard needs to be sweetened.[4]

> The perfection of the world will not be reached until a long time after the creation. Thus God mentions the creation of Man, since his perfection can only come about after long and difficult labour.[5]

The Creation within the six days was only completed to the point where man could take over. This has enormous consequences regarding the task of man in this world: his responsibility to build and cultivate the world became a divine injunction and one of his most important tasks. To be involved in technology, science, and other human endeavors is to be involved in a religious act: a *mitzvah*! The more man fashions the world, the more he fulfills God's command. This, however, means also greater responsibility: The more man knows how to operate and dominate the world, the more he becomes responsible for the consequences—for the outcome, the results of his deeds and creations.

God providing man with fire is, therefore, most significant. He *limits* His own power in order that man may become His partner in the Creation. This self-imposed partial paralysis was to the Greeks an act of divine self-defeat and thus unthinkable.

This Greek worldview is also reflected in early Christianity: While Judaism teaches that God gave man the responsibility of "taking over" and developing the world to its ultimate potential, classical Christianity, which was influenced by the early Greeks, declared man's inability to do anything of the kind. The presumption that man could ever become God's full partner was totally unwarranted. Man, since the days of the Fall in the Garden of Eden, had needed to be liberated from his constant and utter failure. He was helpless and needed to be saved to survive. God's constant and absolute involvement was, therefore, essential. Man cannot do anything but wait for God's salvation and deliverance. This is the underlying motive behind Christianity's principles of incarnation and crucifixion. Since man did not have the strength to come to God, God had to appear in the guise of man and come down to this world to save man from his own failures. Man's inability to stand on his own two feet and bear his own responsibilities and sins caused the need for a substitute to take that responsibility upon his shoulders: through crucifixion.

THE TENT OF MEETING AND THE CREATION

The extent to which God gives man a partnership in all His work is expressed in more than just His call to cultivate and develop the world.

It could be argued that the ultimate expression of God's belief in man's capabilities is shown in the fact that He leaves man with the responsibility of building Him a dwelling place in the form of a Tabernacle. Two matters stand out: First is the striking parallelism between the account of the Creation chapter and the narrative of the construction of the Tabernacle. Second is the unprecedentedly lengthy way in which the Torah records the instructions, the planning, and the actual building of the Sanctuary, and the most concise manner in which the story of the creation of the universe is narrated. The world is created in six days. On the seventh day the Creator "rested" and brought forth an entirely different entity: the Sabbath.

Concerning the construction of the Tabernacle (Exodus 24:16-17) we read again about a sequence of six days consummated by a seventh day:

> Now Moshe went up to the mountain and the cloud covered the mountain. Now the glory of the Lord rested upon Mount Sinai and the cloud covered it for *six* days, and on the *seventh* day He called upon Moshe out of the midst of the cloud. (italics added)

For a span of six days, corresponding to those six primordial days of Creation, Moshe waits in silent anticipation. And again on the seventh day, the Creator once again calls for an entirely new microcosmic matter to come into existence: "Let them make Me a Sanctuary, that I may dwell between them" (Exodus 25:8). However, this time this formation shall be shaped by human hands, not by God. Concerning the Creation, it says (Genesis 1:31): "Now God saw everything He had made and behold it was very good."

In conclusion to the inspection and evaluation of the

Creation, the Torah continues (Genesis 2:3):
blessed the seventh day." Similarly with the Tabernacle: "And Moshe saw all the work, and behold they had done it" (Exodus 39:43). "And Moshe blessed them" (Exodus 39:43).

At the completion of the work of Creation one reads: "Now the Heavens and the Earth and all their hosts were completed and God completed on the seventh day His work which He had made" (Genesis 2:1-2). And again, with the completion of the Tent: "Now was completed all the work of the Tabernacle of the Tent of Meeting" (Exodus 39:32). And: "So Moshe completed the work" (Exodus 40:33).

Man's work on the Tent of Meeting is equated with God creating the universe (note the repetition of the word *completed* in both narratives).[6] Moreover, the Torah devotes nearly *three hundred* verses to the planning and construction of the Tabernacle (not to mention another approximately ninety verses that deal with the garments of the priests officiating in the Tabernacle). Compare this to the chapter on the creation of the world, with less than *thirty-five* verses, from which we may conclude that the Torah is more impressed with man's construction of the Tabernacle than with God creating the entire universe! Most important is the Torah's constant emphasis on the fact that man created the Tabernacle, and *not* God:

> "They will make" . . . and again, "they will make . . . they will make the Sanctuary . . . they will make the curtains . . . they will make the copper altar. . . . "
> "And he made. . . . And he made loops of skyblue wool . . . and he made curtains of goats hair [etc.]." (Exodus, chap. 36)

All this was man-made; there was no divine intervention. We are even told who the people behind the whole operation were: highly skilled men by the names of Bezalel ben Uri and Oholiav ben Ahisamakh.

The Divine Presence was able to dwell there as the result of the work of *man*! *God's presence and future revelation in the world was completely dependent on man making it possible!*

The Jewish view of man's capabilities and potential is not without its problems. The call to become God's partner in creation and the heavy responsibilities that go along with it may give the impression that man could actually measure up to God. The fact that it is left up to man to bring God into this world could easily cause great distortion in man's perception of his place in the world, and hence, failure to appreciate the gap between God and man. This, in turn, could lead to human deification, a not-too-uncommon problem in many ancient and modern societies. Human beings may turn to worship other human beings and power! Were the Greeks and the Christian teachings not right after all when they complained that fire should not be given to man and that man, because of his inadequacy, could not take all this on his shoulders?

SLEEP

One may now be able to understand the midrash mentioned earlier, in which the angels wanted to praise man with exclamations of "Holy." Man endowed with so much power, created in the image of God, and responsible for God's future revelation in the world, they argued, must be equal to God.

What, then, was God to do so as to prevent the deification of all men? Should He retract, calling man inadequate and severing His partnership with him? The Midrash replies:

"God caused sleep to fall on Man, and thus all knew he was [only] a human being."

Sleep destroys the illusion of man's omnipotence and forces man to reconsider his place in the world: he is not totally in control. Every evening he is reminded of his limited powers. During this time, he becomes paralyzed for the sake of God's power! *Sleep heals human grandiosity.*

Sleep, in fact, makes man "wake up" and contemplate daily his newly acquired position. When he wakes up from his sleep, man recognizes that he has not been in control all the time, and yet the world survived! Furthermore, he may once more become amazed at the very world he normally takes for granted. He may once more be impressed by the unprecedented greatness of his Creator.

The dialectic between control and power, on the one hand, and letting go and resting, on the other, is the only way man can find the balance between his obligation to develop, cultivate, create, and dominate, and the possibility of seeing himself as a being without any capability to contribute, struck by his inadequacy and failure to cope with the world.

No doubt, this thought lies behind the mysterious story of Chavah's (Eve's) birth. The Torah informs us that she was created from the rib of Adam *while he was asleep* (Genesis 2:21): One cannot create a successful spiritual relationship with one's partner in life when that relationship is built on power and dominion. Adam, therefore, had to receive his wife while asleep—that is, in surrender!

This may also be the key to a most obscure midrash which tells us that the people of Israel anticipating the *Matan Torah* (receiving the Torah) at Sinai overslept and came too late for this unprecedented and most momentous occasion of all times.[7] This may very well mean that, preparing for this

moment, they withdrew from their creative powers, sur-
rendered, and consequently found themselves, like Adam,
in a sleeping condition, so as to allow the "birth" of the Torah
within their own personalities. Thinking that they could only
receive the Torah within this condition, they nearly "missed"
the *Matan Torah* altogether—which was to teach them that
too much "retreat" would bring their whole purpose as God's
partner into question.

SHABBAT, AN ALERT SLEEP

The directive to develop technology and science is no doubt
a God-given charge and an expression of a divine commitment to the acknowledgment of man's capabilities. The danger that this charge could paradoxically lead to man's usur-
pation of God's role, however, is a real one. Sleep as a daily
reminder of man's limits is, however, not enough to make
man realize this danger.

Sleep itself has to be transformed into an experience that
calls on man to be awake while he sleeps, in order to heighten
his awareness of its significance. What is needed is an "alert
sleep." Hence, immediately after God creates man and en-
joins him to be like the Creator and to fill the earth and
dominate it, God blesses the seventh day and declares it holy
(Genesis 2:3).

On *Shabbat*, man is asked to refrain from the kind of
work that will make him continue to master, form, and develop the world. Once a week man is asked to "sleep while
being awake" so as to understand what it means to be man
standing before God. The halachic (religious legal) notion
of the holiness of *Shabbat*, as described by the Torah, consists of two elements: a restriction on *creative* work and the

need to turn this restriction into a *liberating* act by way of positive, highly educative, and uplifting *Shabbat* customs and imperatives.

THE TENT OF MEETING
AND THE CONCEPT OF WORK

One of the most surprising restrictions on the Sabbath is the restriction on carrying anything in the public domain. In fact, it is the first of thirty-nine forbidden forms of work on the Sabbath, as mentioned in the Oral Tradition.[8] It is also the most discussed human activity in the entire Talmud. What is there in the act of carrying which makes it such a powerful expression of human mastership over the world? Other acts, such as sowing, plowing, building, or creating fire, are easily understood: they are clearly ways through which man masters and cultivates the world. But why should the act of carrying be seen as the ultimate form of human creativity?

A closer look at this reveals that carrying is the very foundation on which all human physical activity is built. Man cannot develop and fashion the world if he does not have the possibility to carry. When man is curtailed from carrying, nearly the whole of human creativity and productivity comes to a standstill. The world finds itself in a universal sleep. By calling on man not to carry in the public domain (the sphere where man's control over the world is most evident), the Torah indirectly interferes in every other human activity: without the possibility of carrying, man can neither plow, build, start a fire, nor control other physical aspects of life.

It is, however, not labor in the usual sense of the word that is forbidden. As mentioned earlier, only that kind of work that represents man's active control over the world is forbidden. Work (*melachah* in Hebrew) is that kind of human activity that is the realization of an idea upon an object through human skill and intelligence in the form of production or the transformation of an object for human use. The prohibition of making fire is not due to the labor required in taking two stones and rubbing them against each other but rather because it represents man's unprecedented mastership over the world. This is *exactly* what the Greeks meant when they said that fire was too powerful a medium to be left in the hands of man. It makes little difference if this power is manifested through making a campfire, turning on an electric light, or driving a car. All of these activities clearly show man's capacity to control.

The Sabbath restrictions set a limit to man's dominion over nature. Nature is transformed from an "it" into a "thou." The world is no longer an object of human gratification. The world gets a raison d'être of its own–it falls back into the hands of its original Creator. On *Shabbat*, every creature, however small, becomes man's equal. It has a right to exist irrespective of its possible use or value to man.

Most striking is the fact that the Oral Tradition derives its definition of work from all the activities required in building the Tabernacle. The thirty-nine forms of forbidden work on *Shabbat* are the very activities that molded the Tent of Meeting:

> To what do these forty but one key works correspond? Rabbi Chanina said: They correspond to the operations for constructing the Tabernacle. There they were sowing, hence you may not sow, they were reaping, hence you may not reap.[9]

Agricultural work (plowing, sowing, reaping, etc.), food preparation (grinding, boiling, kneading, baking, etc.), and craftsmanship (woolwork, weaving, spinning, building, writing, etc.) were all necessary to build the Tabernacle. "They were sowing and reaping to produce the dyes for the various materials; for the dyes they also had to perform many other operations like grinding and kneading."[10]

Looking a little closer, we realize that these activities stand as key activities (*avot melachot*) comprising all purposeful human activity in the physical realm. For example, plowing includes digging, removing stones, fertilizing, and so forth. Baking includes boiling, frying, and melting iron; in other words, it is the general principle that changes the physical or chemical status of a substance by means of heat. In fact, we have here a complete overview of all skillful human creativity.[11]

The Tent of Meeting, then, holds every single form of work through which man shows his unprecedented mastership over the world. By building the Tabernacle, a dwelling place for God, man nearly becomes God's equal. He creates a microcosmos of such perfection that even God can symbolically "fit into it." Man's skillful masterpiece nearly replaces God's own creation!

But even here, paradoxically, is a warning to man to remain humble. Instead of seeing his place in the world as a manifestation of his absolute mastership over all creative powers, he is first called upon to dedicate all his creative talents towards a higher goal: the Tent of Meeting. First, as in the case of the first fruits to be offered in the Temple, before man is permitted to fully enjoy all his talents, he is asked to give the "firstlings (*maaser*) of all these talents to His God and Creator. Only *after* the dedication of all his talents to the

Tabernacle can he really start to use these very talents to build and master the world.

SHABBAT, AN ACT OF LIBERATION

An often-made mistake is to believe that the thirty-nine forms of forbidden work are just restrictive and burdensome. This is far from true, and it shows a lack of insight into human psychology. Indeed, they are liberating, making man into a free and independent being. Man's dedication to the advancement and building of the world could easily turn him into a slave of his own mastership and talents. Man's tendency to become a workaholic overwhelmed by his own power could easily make him prisoner of this very power:

> Man has become a superman . . . , but the superman with superhuman power has not risen to superhuman reason. To the degree to which his power grows he becomes more and more a poor man. . . . It must shake up our conscience that we become all the more inhuman the more we grow into supermen.[12]

The more man busies himself with creating the world around him, the less chance he has to "create" himself. The more he focuses his creative talents on the external world, the smaller the chance that he will be introspective and contemplate his own place in this world and the need to grow spiritually. Instead of mastering his own creative talents, these talents start controlling him and turn him into an obsessive and imprisoned being.

By barring all creative activities (as described above) on

the Sabbath, man is liberated from these often-possessive talents and thus breathes more freely. It is as though these creative activities are not really curtailed or paralyzed but rather are refocused onto man himself. By putting the external creative activities on hold, man can now start building and fashioning himself into a better and more dignified person. He now has a chance to focus on his marriage, his family, and his friends and take notice of nature (which stands now equal to him). He can now start mastering himself. By being prohibited from picking up the phone (a most disturbing intruder into his personal life), man is provided with free time to rethink his relationship with his Maker and fellowman. When a flower cannot be plucked, this God-given creation becomes a "thou" and makes man realize the very existence and dignity of nature.

Freedom does not mean that people do whatever they like to do. Rather, freedom means growing spiritually within those guidelines that afford man the possibility to realize his potential. No laissez-faire, no arbitrariness: freedom means obedience to the laws that govern optimal human development.

The thirty-nine forbidden activities could therefore be called "prohibitions toward genuine liberty." The time that has become free is now used for uplifting experiences such as *Kiddush* (sanctification of the day), festive meals, *zemirot* (*Shabbat* songs), study, reading, and discussions about the portion of the Torah that is read in the synagogue service; relaxation; playing with children or grandchildren, and so forth. Once a week, man experiences the Garden of Eden in his own home and surroundings.

Erich Fromm, one of the world's most influential thinkers on psychological, philosophical, and social issues, writes about the Sabbath:

The Sabbath is the most important of the biblical concepts, and of later Judaism. It is the only strictly religious command in the Ten Commandments: Its fulfillment is insisted upon by the otherwise anti-ritualistic prophets; it was a most strictly observed commandment throughout 2,000 years of Diaspora life, wherein its observation often was hard and difficult. It can hardly be doubted that the Sabbath was the fountain of life for the Jews, who, scattered, powerless and often despised and persecuted, renewed their pride and dignity when like kings they celebrated the Sabbath. Is the Sabbath nothing but a day of rest in the mundane sense of freeing people, at least on one day, from the burden of work? To be sure it is that, and this function gives it the dignity of one of the great innovations in human evolution. Yet if this were all that it was, the Sabbath would hardly have played the central role I have just described. In order to understand this role we must penetrate to the core of the Sabbath institution. It is not rest per se in the sense of not making an effort, physically or mentally. It is rest in the sense of the re-establishment of complete harmony between human beings and between them and nature. Nothing must be destroyed and nothing must be built: the Sabbath is a day of truce in the human battle with the world, even tearing up a blade of grass is looked upon as a breach of this harmony, as is lighting a match. Neither must social change occur. It is for this reason that carrying anything on the street is forbidden (even if it weighs as little as a handkerchief) while carrying a heavy load in one's garden is permitted. The point is not that the effort of carrying a load is forbidden, but the transfer of any object from one privately owned piece of land to another, because such transfer constituted, originally, a transfer of property. On the Sabbath one lives as if one *has* nothing, pursuing no aim except *being*, that is expressing one's essential powers: praying, studying, eating, drinking, singing, making love. The Sabbath is a day of joy because on that day one is fully oneself. This is the reason that the Talmud calls the Sabbath the anticipation of the messianic times, and the messianic time the unending Sabbath: the day on which property and money as well as mourning and sadness are taboo; a day on which time is defeated and pure being rules. . . . The modern Sunday is a day of fun, consumption, and running away from oneself. *One might ask if it is not time to reestablish the Sabbath as a universal day of harmony and peace, as the human day that anticipates the human future.* (italics added)[13]

HAVDALAH

On Saturday night, when man is called upon by God to become once more His partner in the Creation, man is first of all asked to create fire, the key to all human development.[14] Only when he has reenacted Adam's first creative act and pronounces Adam's blessing over this fire does God once more permit him to use all his creative talents on the external world. (This is the reason behind the old custom at the *Havdalah* ceremony to hold one's hands closed up to a special flame, only to open them a moment later: First, one keeps the fingers closed to express the idea that up till now, man's hands were tied because they were not allowed to be involved in physical constructive activity. Now, with conclusion of the Sabbath and by the medium of fire, man is again free to actively work with his hands—hence the opening of the fingers [Rabbi Meir of Rothenburg].) Imbued with the experience of the Sabbath, man reenters into the world of science and development—only now, his participation in building the world becomes a *mitzvah*, a religious deed!

RELIGIOUS OBSESSION

In the middle of the biblical narrative concerning the actual construction of the Tabernacle, we read about a most surprising incident. When the Israelites started to bring their contributions to be used in the building of the Sanctuary and the "men of skill" started their work, the latter suddenly stopped work and walked up to Moshe with the following complaint:

> "The people are bringing more than is needed for the task entailed in the work that the Lord has commanded to be done." Moshe thereupon had this proclamation made throughout the camp: "Let no man or woman make further effort toward gifts for the Sanctuary!" So the people stopped bringing. For their efforts had been more than enough to carry out all the work, and there [even] remained some left over. (Exodus 36:4-7)

Some strong questions come to mind: Why would "the men of skill" stop their work in the middle of the day to tell Moshe that the people brought more than was needed? Could they not have waited until the evening, when they were coming home from a hard day's work? Why did Moshe proclaim an immediate and complete stop to all contributions, as if he foresaw a great calamity? Why does this story get such a comprehensive hearing? Instead, the Torah could have told this all in one sentence: "And the people brought too much and Moshe stopped them."

The story seems to speak of some sort of panic that befell the men of skill and Moshe.

Careful observation may, however, reveal to us that the panic reaction on the part of the men of skill was not without foundation. When Moshe asked the people to contribute to the building of the Sanctuary (Exodus 25), the people, in their enthusiasm, got "carried" away and kept on bringing more without end. The hasty and careless running of the people to bring as much as possible sounded the wrong trumpet to the "men of skill." They realized that the people, in their desire to contribute (and, perhaps, to outdo each other), lost themselves and were no longer capable of acknowledging and appreciating the very special nature of this operation. The construction of the Tabernacle is, first and foremost, a matter of the condition of the heart. It is the *kavanah* (intention) that counts, not just the act of contribution. To build the Sanctuary is, above all, a matter of quality, and not of quantity. When it became clear that the Israelites were overwhelmed and obsessed with the "importance" of their contribution, Moshe and the men of skill realized that the most important ingredient, the contrition of the heart towards the proper building of the Tabernacle, was lost and totally ignored. They concluded that the Israelites were no longer building the "dwelling place" of God but rather an ordinary tent with no spiritual dimensions.

As such, this activity had to be stopped immediately, before the Tent of Meeting turned into a tent of idol worship—in other words, a tent that symbolically pretended to hold the *Shechinah*, the Divine Presence, but in fact could not.

In light of this we may now understand why God informed Moshe to tell the Israelites to observe *Shabbat* while building the Sanctuary. No doubt, the Tabernacle symbolizes God's constant presence in the midst of man, but how will man remind himself of this if he does not take time to pause and contemplate? *The very building of the Sanctuary may turn into an obsession–a religious obsession, a Golden Calf*! The institution of *Shabbat* makes man take a step back. A moment of contemplation and introspection guarantees that he is on the right track and not the victim of a religious deception.

3

On Jewish Identity and the Chosen People

ne of the most disturbing claims ever made by men is the one that Jews make when, quoting the Bible, they insist on being the Chosen People. For nearly four thousand years, Jews have upheld the belief that they are God's elect, the "apple of His eye," His most beloved and favored nation. This belief expresses itself in a peculiar Covenant consisting of laws and regulations emphasizing the unprecedented relationship between God, the Creator of the universe, and the small nation of Israel, to the exclusion of everybody else.

Instead of being embarrassed by this claim, Jews have, in general, been rather proud of it. Jewish literature throughout the ages has given much weight to this claim. Rabbis and Sages have done everything to strengthen this belief, giving Jews the feeling that they are a species apart.

FAVORITISM

Indeed, it cannot be doubted that this seems to be one of the most dangerous claims ever made by human beings. Saying that the Jews are the Chosen People is saying that a people that does not even make up 1 percent of the human race is more precious than, and superior to, any other people. If less than 1 percent of all men are chosen, then more than 99 percent are not! This sounds like prejudice of the highest order, making the vast majority of mankind into second-class citizens of the world.

Such claims obviously ask for great trouble. Many a war has broken out because of these kinds of credenda. How often have nations fought and tried to destroy each other on the basis of claims of superiority?

In fact, the Jews' insistence on being the Chosen People has often been blamed for the making of similar claims by other nations and races. Ever since that day, the world has seen the most outrageous forms of human suffering. Millions have lost their lives because others believed in their own chosenness and superiority.

Looking into the history of the Japanese we see how this nation caused unbelievable anguish to others in the name of a peculiar credo of elitism. The English, as well as many other nations, have also had their share in claiming to be "chosen." But without any doubt, the Germans of modern time outdid all earlier nations with their atrocities. With their philosophy of the *Herrenvolk* (Master People), they declared war on all minorities, nations, and ethnic groups. Since the day when they claimed ultimate superiority, no human being has been safe. We are reminded of Nietzsche's statement that Germans saw themselves as *Uebermenschen* (supermen), and as such, capable of causing unlimited harm to their fellow-men.

Carl Gustav Jung, the famous Swiss psychiatrist, warned in 1936 of the incredible dangers inherent in the German national character, which could ultimately lead to the destruction of millions of people:

The symptoms are evident in Germany, the emphasis on the Germanic, i.e., Aryan, race on blood and soil. . . . [They show that] their house is filled with "a mighty wind." . . . A wild, irrational power has broken out in Germany, while we still believe that the weather is following its normal course. . . . Germany is a land of spiritual catastrophes. . . . It seizes everything which is in its way and uproots anything that is not firmly rooted. When the wind blows, all insecurity, outward or inward, is revealed. . . . We cannot imagine as yet, but we can expect [these catastrophes] to appear in the course of the next years or decades.[1]

The famous English author George Bernard Shaw accused the Jews of arrogance and stated that as long as they kept on insisting upon their chosenness, they had no right to object and protest against the monstrous way in which the Germans had killed six million of their people. In fact, the Jews had brought disaster upon themselves, including the Holocaust!

H. G. Wells called the Jewish claim "a hindrance to world unity." Protestant theologians spoke about "the haughtiness of Jewish belief in which the Jewish God was only interested in protecting His own people."

In the notorious "Protocols of Zion," Jews are accused of world domination. Theirs was the scandal of "particularity," which was considered an "absurd" pretension.

Arnold Toynbee, the famous historian, is totally unreserved in his criticism of the Jewish credo: "The most notorious historical example of idolization of an ephemeral self is the error of the Jews. . . . They persuaded themselves that Israel's discovery of the One True God had revealed Israel itself to be God's Chosen People."[2]

Indeed, a careful look into the Jewish tradition shows a marked emphasis on Jewish particularity and the need to create even thicker walls between Jews and non-Jews. There is the prohibition against marrying a non-Jew, which forbids any Jew to marry a non-Jew, regardless of skin color, race, or social background! It tolerates no exceptions or compromises. It draws a deep divide between Jews and non-Jews.

Does this not imply that gentiles are not good enough for Jews to marry? Not even the Germans could think of such a radical step! For Judaism mixed marriages are insufferable and considered a flat denial of everything Jewish. A Jew marrying a non-Jewish partner is seen as an act of treason. It is the final and most brazen act of rebellion on the part of the Jew. Most of the time, such a move leads to the ostracism of the Jewish partner from all forms of Jewish communal life.

Neither does the Jewish tradition see any reason to try and convert non-Jews. In fact, it greatly discourages such steps. It is only with the greatest reluctance that the Jewish faith is prepared to "take in" gentiles. The Covenant is particular and therefore exclusive.

Others have already noted that the institution of *Kashrut* (the dietary laws) was introduced with the express purpose of drawing a distinction between Jews and gentiles. Jews cannot, for the most part, eat of the food of non-Jews or drink their wines. This obviously limits social intercourse to a great extent, and as such functions as another successful way of preventing mixed marriages.

On *Motsaei Shabbat*, Saturday night after the Sabbath comes to an end, another ceremony makes it clear that Jews and gentiles have little in common. At the *Havdalah* ceremony, which makes a distinction between the Sabbath and the rest of the (profane) week, the major domus takes a glass of wine in his hand and declares: "Praised is God . . . who makes a distinction between that which is holy [the Sabbath] and the profane [the rest of the week]" and then continues to praise Him as He "who makes a distinction between Israel and the nations of the world"!

One could add to this that Jews have always striven to live on their own, apart from the rest of the gentile community, deliberately dressing differently, speaking their own language (Ladino/Yiddish), and creating their own completely unique customs, prayers, and culture.

It is therefore not surprising that Jews themselves have called for the elimination of the doctrine of Jewish Chosenness. The Hebrew writer J. H. Brenner wrote: "I would blot out from the prayer book of the Jews of our day the 'Thou hast chosen us' in every shape and form."[3]

The famous Jewish thinker and founder of the Jewish Reconstructionist movement, Mordechai Kaplan, whose pride in his Jewishness cannot be doubted, had a similar message: he believed that the concept of chosenness is incompatible with democracy and the equality and dignity of all men. With the publication of the Reconstructionist prayer book, he added, "Modern-minded Jews can no longer believe . . . that the Jews constitute a divinely chosen people".[4]

EQUALITY OF ALL MEN

In view of what we mentioned above, what strikes us as paradoxical is the fact that traditional Judaism has gone out of its way to stress the dignity of *all* men. When reading the Creation chapter we are told that (long before Jews ever appeared on the globe) *all* men were created in the Image of God, and not just some distinctive people (Genesis, chap. 1).

The Prophet's words are clear: "Have we not all one Father, has not one God created us?" (Malachi 2:10).

Rabbi Meir stated that Adam was created from dust that had been collected from all corners of the earth so that no nation could claim the distinction of being better or having cradled mankind.[5]

In later Jewish tradition, we read that God created all men from one couple so that nobody could claim "that one race is better than another."[6] Non-Jews who study the Torah are compared to the high priest.[7]

One is reminded of Rabbi Israel of Kotnitz's prayer concerning the non-Jews:

> Lord of the Universe, I beg you to redeem Israel, but if You do not want to do that, then I beg you, redeem the gentiles.

Despite the fact that Judaism definitely does not encourage non-Jews to convert, it does insist that *all* gentiles *can* convert to Judaism and be part of the People of Israel. Looking into Jewish history we find some of the greatest personalities to be descendants of non-Jews. King David is a descendant of a woman called Ruth from the nation of Moab. One of Israel's archenemies, this nation was known for its sexual immorality. Rabbi Akiva, the most important Sage of the second century, had as his forefathers non-Jews who converted to Judaism. So had Shamaya and Avtalyon—outstanding Sages of the first century. Onkelos the Proselyte (second century), the author of the most authoritative translation of the Torah in the Aramaic language, was the son of the sister of Titus. He is seen as one the greatest Torah scholars that Judaism has ever known.

The Jewish message to pray and wait for the most "universal" man of all—the *mashiach* (messiah), is a profound statement for universal concern and brotherhood. This man, who personifies all that Jews have been dreaming of, carries much gentile blood. A descendant of David and, consequently, of Ruth the Moabite, the *mashiach*'s ancestry includes many gentiles. Judaism declared this personality as the most righteous man on earth and the ultimate redeemer of all mankind.

But should the need arise to demonstrate Judaism's total condemnation of racism, a study of the "law of the Amalekite" would prove helpful. As is known, the Amalekites are seen as the most dangerous and notorious enemies of the Jews. Their constant and highly successful attacks on the People of Israel, their deep hate for anything Jewish, were so great that Jews received a divine instruction never to forget their animosity and to "blot out the memory" of all Amalekites (Exodus 17:14-16; Deuteronomy 25:17-19). The Amalekite became the prototype of all anti-Semites.

This created a major dilemma within Jewish religious law: What if an Amalekite should wish to convert to Judaism? This would be comparable to a Nazi asking to become a Jew! For many people, the thought alone would be appalling. The answer is therefore without precedent: *An Amalekite (as long as he himself did not kill) should be accepted in the community of Israel.*[8] This is boldness of the first order!

THE PARADOX OF TRADITION

We are confronted with a most amazing situation. On the one hand, we have observed how much Judaism has tried to erect walls between Jews and gentiles, how much it wants to secure Israel's chosenness. On the other hand, we are told that the equality of all men, the dignity of all human beings, is the cornerstone upon which all traditional Judaism stands. In the face of such contradictory statements, we would immediately exclaim that Judaism is guilty of double standards.

We may henceforth observe that Judaism seems to incorporate a most confusing paradox. Like other monotheistic religions, its God is universal, but *unlike* any other, its Covenant is particular. No gentile is encouraged to join, but just like every Jew, the gentile *is* created in the image of God. This is perplexing enough.

It is, however, the scope of Jewish law as the expression of the particular Covenant between God and Israel that is even more problematic. Many of its laws include a demand for moral behavior and seem to be built on the principles of the most advanced ethics. No doubt many of them apply in relationship to humanity at large, but others only apply to the Community of Israel, such as no interest charge on a loan (Deuteronomy 23:20), taking care of a neighbor's lost property (Deuteronomy 22:1-3), and priorities in saving somebody's life (Leviticus 19:16).[9]

Judaism also claims that many of its rituals, such as *Shabbat* observance, the festivals, and sexual purity, have great ethical value. Why, then, do these laws not apply to gentiles? Why deprive them of such obligations?

In fact, we touch here on one of the most biting criticisms of Judaism in modern times. In his famous work *Groundwork of the Metaphysics of Morals*, the German philosopher Immanuel Kant argues for the idea that a moral judgment must be universal in scope. We must, says Kant, be able to will that a maxim of our action should become a universal law. Otherwise, there is moral inconsistency.[10]

This seems to run against the very essence of a divine moral law as found in the Jewish tradition. Judaism is an ethical system for a particular people. Seen from the perspective of Kant, therefore, Judaism fails the test of morality. What is the solution to this paradox?

HISTORICAL REALITY

Before we can try to find an answer to this paradox, we must first of all prevent falling into a major trap. It has become very clear that nowadays any philosophy, however dangerous, can be justified. Nazism and its underlying philosophy, however cruel and outrageous, is a case in point. Nazis have constantly argued that their war against the Jews was not only justifiable but morally obligatory: Jews and others had to be destroyed if mankind were ever to have a better chance of succeeding. (Only a superior breed of mankind, like the Germans, could guarantee a better future for all men!)

In light of this we must be very careful not to propose arguments that are, in fact, nothing but apologetic and dangerous ideologies. This is especially true when we are discussing matters as sensitive as "chosenness."

What, then, are our guarantees not to fall into this kind of trap? We can only suggest one criterion: empirical evidence as reflected in current and historical reality. Reality, after all, cannot easily be rejected or ignored. It is the most reliable gauge we have (even though some philosophers have tried to cast doubts on the reliability of reality!).

In our case, we must therefore ask an important question: Does historical *reality* confirm the unique status of the People of Israel, does it say anything about Jews being different that may offer some support to the Jewish traditional approach of chosenness? Is there anything about the People of Israel that does not just confirm its different culture and history but sets it apart, far beyond the normal, conventional differences between one nation and another?

Our answer must be clearly in the affirmative. A recognition of cold historical facts proves most revealing: the Jewish People stand out in three matters.

1. It experienced a most miraculous survival.
2. It made a totally unprecedented return to its homeland after nearly two thousand years of exile.
3. It has made most outstanding contributions to Western civilization, totally out of proportion to the actual sum total of its populace.

A Most Miraculous Survival

The Jewish People is, without doubt, one of the oldest nations of the world. No nation has seen so much exile and suffering. The years that the nation of Israel spent peacefully in the Land of Israel are few compared to the thousands of years it had to live in *galut* (exile). Their suffering was beyond all imagination:

> If there are ranks in suffering, Israel takes precedence of all the nations; if the duration of sorrows and the patience with which they are borne ennoble, the Jews can challenge the aristocracy of every land; if a literature is called rich in the possession of few classic tragedies—what shall we say to a national tragedy lasting for fifteen hundred years in which the poets and the actors were also the heroes?[11]

Combine all the woes that temporal tyrannies have ever inflicted on men or nations and all have fallen short of the full measure of suffering that the People of Israel has endured century after century. The never-ending conspiracy to exterminate the members of this people is without comparison in human records.

Its history in the Land during biblical times was short, it was surrounded by nations that were committed to the destruction of its State; war after war did the Jews have to wage, only to endure even more animosity. Afterward, they were sent into their longest exile. There, it became the "mission" of many a nation to do everything to make the lives of the Jewish People hell on earth. Beaten, killed, tortured, the Jew was expelled from one country to another, only to find another disaster awaiting him.

The Jew became the scapegoat for national and social hysteria. Still, he survived six empires: the Egyptians, the Babylonians, the Persians, the Greeks, the Romans and, lately, the Germans.

He was discriminated against, put behind ghetto walls and bars, excluded from social intercourse, forbidden from entering into the bastions of the academic world, and economically, consistently outlawed. He was constantly dying but . . . never died. Reduced to a small percentage of his original membership, he stayed alive and *outlived* all his enemies. Instead of succumbing, he did the impossible: he became stronger and eventually stood at the graveside of nearly all of his enemies. The Jews saw them all, beat them all, and continued what they had always been doing: enduring and going on with their peculiar way of life.

They violated all the rules of history, "ridiculed" the most sophisticated and highly appraised theories concerning history, and became, for this reason, either the *most annoying* or the *most celebrated people* of the world.

I remember how the materialist interpretation of history, when I attempted in youth to verify it by applying it to destinies of peoples, broke down in the case of the Jews, where destiny seemed absolutely inexplicable from the materialistic standpoint. And indeed according to the materialistic and positive criterion this people ought long ago to have perished. Its survival is a mysterious and wonderful phenomenon demonstrating that the life of this people is governed by a special predetermination, transcending the processes of adaptation expounded by the materialistic interpretation of history. The survival of the Jews, their resistance to destruction, their endurance under absolutely peculiar conditions and the fateful role played by them in history; all these point to the particular and mysterious foundations of their destiny.[12]

The Jews' Return to Their Homeland

Not only did the Jews survive in the face of all their suffering, they even managed to free themselves of their nearly two-thousand-year-old exile to return to the land of their forefathers! Just moments after they had experienced their worst destruction, the Holocaust, Jews picked up their bags and "went home."

Shortly after they had lost nearly two million of their children, the future of any nation, Jews fought a battle to free their land of their many enemies, and succeeded. At a time when the whole world declared that there was no longer a future for the Jew, the State of Israel appeared—as if from nowhere.

The return of the Jews to their homeland is, therefore, a totally unprecedented event, an event sui generis. No nation, after a two-thousand-year-long road of pogroms, liquidations, and holocausts, ever returned to its homeland and built, successfully (and within forty-five years), a completely modern state (including a very sophisticated army and a high-tech science program).

It is a phenomenon totally unheard of, breaking all conventional criteria and violating all principles of conformity. There is no analogous event in all of history: to many it became an international embarrassment, to others, a reason for jubilation.

Outstanding Contributions

Jews have had an overpowering grip over human minds and hearts. They should, however, never have been heard of, being many times weaker in number than the smallest tribes in Africa. But instead of being "a nebulous dim puff of star dust in the blaze of the milky way"[13] they have contributed to the world in every possible and "impossible" way.

They brought monotheism to this world—the most powerful idea man has ever heard of. Since that day the universe has never been the same. The gift of the Bible to the world turned all human deeds into moral actions and responsibilities, teaching ethics and justice. Furthermore, the Jews gave birth to the New Testament and, for the Christians, to a man they believe to be the messiah, bringing about a world religion. No Koran could have existed without the Jews, and no international or American law could have become what it is today, were it not for the contributions of Jewish religious thought.

In later centuries Jews contributed to scientific technology, literature, music, finance, medicine, and art, all this in ways far beyond anybody's expectations of a small, tortured people. They were involved in many social revolutions, often becoming leaders and thinkers. They produced Maimonides,

Nachmanides, the Gaon of Vilna, and thousands of illustrious Sages, religious thinkers, and legalists.

Even when they started to assimilate, they managed to produce people like Spinoza, Freud, Einstein, and other geniuses who revolutionized the world.

> [The Jews] were here before us, they are our elders. Their children were taught to read from the scrolls of the Torah before our Latin alphabet reached its final form. . . . As compared with the Jews we are young; we are newcomers; in the matter of civilization they are far ahead of us. It was in vain that we locked them up for several hundred years behind the walls of the Ghetto. No sooner were their prison gates unbarred than they easily caught up with us, even on those paths which we opened up without their aid.[14]

It is abundantly clear, therefore, that the Jew has taken a most unusual place in the history of nations. He does not fit into any conventional pattern. He transcends all categories that scientists and sociologists have devised: "The Jewish people represent a sociologically unique phenomenon and defy all attempts at general definition."[15]

Having observed all this, we may now confidently state that Jews are indeed "a nation apart." The claim that they are different is not just a theory but is deeply rooted in their very history and communal experience.

THE TOWER OF BABEL

Now that we have established that Jews have an unequaled and extraordinary historical experience, we may turn to our original question: has the doctrine of Chosenness anything to do with this?

Our first task is to turn to the source from which this claim of chosenness originates: the Torah and, in particular, those chapters that take us through the days preceding the appearance of the first Jew, called Avraham.

Chapter 11 in Genesis is our first choice. In this chapter we read about the unusual story of a world population that is caught between tranquillity and agitation, peace and uneasiness:

> And the whole earth was one language and of uniform words. And it came to pass as they journeyed from the east that they found a plain in the land of Shinar and they settled there. And they said one to the other: Come let us make bricks and burn them thoroughly. . . . And they said: Come let us build us a city and a tower, with its top in heaven and let us make ourselves a name; lest we be scattered about upon the face of the earth. (Genesis 11:1-5)

All this takes place after mankind has experienced its first holocaust in the form of the Flood, which only Noach and his family had survived.

The story continues to tell us that God was far from "pleased" with this new undertaking. "And the Lord said: 'Behold they are one people and they all have one language, and this is what they begin to do . . . !'" (11:6). This is followed by a most unusual divine response—God decides to bring confusion upon man by mixing up his language, "so that one man may not understand his neighbor. So the Lord scattered them about upon the face of all the earth" (7-8).

This story, one of the shortest in the whole of the *Tanach* (Bible), is most puzzling.

1. Why did mankind, living in tranquillity, speaking one language and uniform words, suddenly see the need to move

to the east, later known as Babylon (Iraq and Iran)? The
lack of space could not have been the problem: All of the
earth was still empty after the great noachide holocaust;
people could easily have taken more land without the need
for a complete dislodgment from their original location?
2. What does it mean that they spoke one language and *also*
"uniform words"? Which language was this and what are
"uniform words"?
3. Why did God not agree to this new enterprise? What
could possibly be wrong in building a new environment
made from bricks and erecting a tower, and thereby creating better conditions for men?
4. Why did God end this episode with the "mixing of languages" (Babel)? Were there no other ways of stopping
this undertaking? Why did He select language?

NIMROD

In order to fully comprehend the biblical narrative, one
should always analyze the chapter preceding. In our case we
have to turn to chapter 10. Amongst many things, chapter
10 tells us about a man called Nimrod, a rather violent personality, who seems to have played a major role in the up-
coming events: "And Cush begat Nimrod, he began to be a
mighty man in the land. He was a mighty hunter before God.
. . . And the beginning of his kingdom was Babel" (10:8-10).

This narrative seems to be about the first despot. Rashi
(10:8) in his commentary inquires about the origin of his
name.

"[Why is he called Nimrod?] Because he caused the whole
world to rebel [Lehamrid-Nimrod] against the Holy One

blessed be He, by advising [suggesting to] them concerning the generation of the division of mankind, [to build the Tower and cause the world to be divided by a language barrier]."

A little later Rashi comments on the reason Nimrod is called a "hunter": "He captures [hunts] the minds of men with his mouth and leads them to rebel against the Omnipresent."[16]

Here a major accusation is being made: Nimrod manipulates the minds of the men of his generation; he traps them by way of his words and indoctrinates them, with the purpose of bringing about a mass rebellion against God, the Creator and Sustainer of the world.

Radak (Rabbi David Kimchi, 1160-1236) adds: "He began to show his might to conquer one or more peoples and to become king over them. For till he arose no man had aspired to rule over a people."[17]

The picture that slowly emerges is one of a man who, completely obsessed by himself, tries and succeeds in getting all mankind to succumb to his wishes. Nimrod, being a "mighty man" and originally a hunter of huge animals (Abravanel) suddenly realizes that his fellowmen are afraid of him and no longer dare to oppose him for fear of death.

Slowly but surely he succeeds in rallying people around him and forces them to acknowledge him as their king. But this is insufficient for his ego. With great urgency he convinces them that he is their new god, to be served and celebrated. This leads to an ultimate break with the monotheistic belief in one omnipresent God: the God of monotheism has to be exiled from men's thoughts and aspirations.

Once this God is ignored or even denied, moral obligations and the need for justice are no longer required: might is right. Obsessed with his own *amour propre*, Nimrod has to ensure that his fellowmen will see themselves as his servants and slaves, denying their own selves and succumbing to anything that he, the new god, may demand.

This is only possible when the monotheistic God is once and for all done away with. Nimrod, then, must perforce be seen as the forerunner of all the dictators and manipulators of history: he was the first Hitler, Stalin, or Lenin. This, as the reader shall see later, is symptomatic of the story: It is remarkable in its similarity with modern times.

The leitmotiv behind the story is not the actual building of this new society but rather a most disturbing element underlying it—the desire to invest human aspirations to grandeur in one man. This is also the reason behind the erection of the Tower of Babel with its "peak into heaven." Nimrod, obsessed with his divinity, needs to destroy his great "rival," God! The tower is the means to reach that goal. In his utterly simplistic belief he has to go to heaven to fight God and kill Him. He views God as being no more than "an old man with a long white beard," running the heavens and the earth. When Nimrod gets his well-trained army to ascend to heaven by climbing the tower, he will have made a major step forward. Once God is killed, Nimrod's dream of world domination will be well on its way.

ONE LANGUAGE AND UNIFORM WORDS

We are, however, left with a paradox. The opening words of the chapter give a very different impression to that delineated above: "And the whole of the earth was of one language and of uniform words" (11:1-2).

A generation of brotherhood and peace! How can this

be? Could the self-obsessed man Nimrod have been the mastermind behind such tranquillity? Is he to be praised for having created a most advanced society in which all men were in agreement? This question becomes even more acute when we realize the meaning of the words "one language and uniform words." Most commentaries are of the opinion that "one language" means the Holy Language—classical Hebrew—while "uniform words" means a spiritual mental agreement, one weltanschauung, one ideology.[18]

In other words, not only was there one language spoken (Hebrew) but people even managed to think and express themselves in a similar ideology, with no disagreements, arguments, or opposing philosophies!!

In a most surprising midrash, we are carefully informed about the reasons and implications of this:[19]

> [What is the meaning of *devarim achadim* (uniform words)?] It means that what belonged to one person, belonged also to his neighbor and that what belonged to his neighbor belonged also to him. They possessed everything together, had one partnership and one communal purse.

The similarity with modern times is striking: communism and socialism! Somehow our story introduces us to the first forms of social reform and human equality. But on a deeper level, we may very well see some allusions to Kant's "Universal Moral Law." To achieve the goals of universal equality, Nimrod, like Kant, believed in the establishment of a moral law that would draw no distinctions between people. It had to be applicable to all people under all circumstances with no exception.

Although one must admit that communism was not the greatest of blessings, nonetheless, the driving force behind it was the desire for a better world. This has also been the underlying motive behind the great social reformers of modern times. Without wanting to give too much credit to Nimrod, one still wonders if he was not the forerunner of Karl Marx and Friedrich Engels, the creators of modern socialism and the authors of the *Communist Manifesto*.

The same is true regarding Nimrod's introduction of the Kantian philosophy of a universal moral law. While admitting that Kant failed in creating a better world order through his moral code (to be discussed later), one cannot, however, doubt his sincere intentions. So why condemn Nimrod as one of the most evil characters in human history when he tried to accomplish the very ideas suggested by these great men many thousands of years later?

THE NOACHIDE HOLOCAUST

This question becomes even more forceful if one takes note of the situation that brought about the noachide flood, which preceded the story of Nimrod. What did that generation do wrong that it brought upon itself such calamity in terms of the Flood? The story leaves no doubt: "The land was corrupted before God and the land was filled with *chamas* [violence]" (6:11). *Chamas*, Rashi informs us, is not just violence in general; it is robbery, the violation of private property.

One can very well understand why, some generations later, mankind was still small and frail and did not want to cause a second flood. Consequently man removed any possibility for discontentment and robbery. Learning from the mistakes of the preceding generation, men decided in favor of a social system that made the violation of private property impossible, a system in which all men would share all the

possessions, and in which one universal law would be bind-
ing on all.

If so, one may exclaim in sheer wonderment: Why was
this generation identified with dictatorship and evil, bringing about the need for divine intervention? They appear to
have drawn the correct conclusion from the mistakes of their
grandparents and repented, creating better conditions. They
should be admired for their courage. Why not give Nimrod
the benefit of the doubt instead of portraying him as an ancient Hitler?

INDEPENDENCE OF NATURE

A more careful analysis of the story draws yet another incident to notice. At the beginning of the story, it says that this
"second" generation of "flood survivors" "journeyed from the
east, and found a plain [bik'a] in the land of Shinar, and there
they dwelled" (11:2).

As before, the question arises, why did they move?
Surely, as stated earlier, it was not from lack of space; the
growing population only had to broaden its borders. There
was no need for a move en masse. What is even more surprising is the location on which they finally settled. They
found a bik'a, which is a gap or a cleft. There were no mountains, no forest, no agriculture, no natural resources. What
could have been the reason behind such a move—coming
from a place that had much more to offer, where the surroundings were definitely more pleasant?

This is where we are introduced to Nimrod's genius.
Realizing that it would be no easy task to get his people to
believe in his divinity, Nimrod had to make a forceful impression on everybody. He had to prove his ability to replace

the former celebrated God, his great rival. He had to show his independence of this God and, therefore, of nature as well. His objective was very clear: he would take "his" people to the most unsuitable place he could think of, a place without any resources, only sand and unlivable circumstances. And out of all this he would create, single-handedly, a most sophisticated and highly developed society. Nothing given by nature would assist him; nowhere would there be a trace of this "all-powerful God"! He, Nimrod, would demonstrate his own divinity: a creatio ex nihilo!

This would be a fortress of human power. Built with bricks, mortar, and clay, it would become the metropolis of the future. Based on the latest scientific and technological discoveries, it would express the glorious manifestation of man's strength, reflecting Algernon Charles Swinburne's "Glory to man in the highest, the maker and master of things" ("Hymn to Man"):

> And they said one to other: Come let us make bricks and burn them thoroughly. And they had brick for stone and mortar they had for clay. And they said: *Come let us build us a city and a tower, with its top into heaven and let us make ourselves a name.* (Genesis 11:3-4) (italics added)

It was *not* the need and desire to build a better society for women and children that motivated them; it was the urge for prestige and power, fame and glory, impressing upon the many generations to come and see the accomplishments of the earlier generations. *This* became the great catalyst behind Nimrod's dream: *Let us make ourselves a name!*

The bricks show us that these are misguided people, who imagine the world to be fixed reality, people in whom material desire is dominant. Such were the people who concentrated all their energies into the building of the Tower of Babel, one huge fortress of worldliness dedicated to the greater satisfaction of man's temporal needs, a monument of humanist extremism.[20]

Nimrod had ultimately reached his goal. Mankind, enraptured by his overpowering personality and power-ideology, had become completely "taken in" by the bizarre philosophy of a man who thought only of himself. Like Hitler and Stalin, Nimrod had succeeded in portraying himself as "the savior of the people." Promising a better future for his people, with comfort, joy, and prestige, he had in fact turned them into his slaves and denied them a sense of dignity and self-esteem.

Just as in Nazi Germany, mankind had ultimately adopted its dictator's philosophy and made it its own. It believed Nimrod's ideology to be the highest good; it identified with it and was prepared to die for it!

CENTRALIZATION

It is no longer difficult to understand God's disapproval of this generation. Indoctrinated by Nimrod, they *started* to speak *devarim achadim*, words showing that they had adopted a philosophy of *artificial* fraternity. The error and sin of Nimrod was not the building of the city and the tower but the use of these artificial means in order to force *Centralization* or, in modern parlance, *Totalitarianism* on his people. For many naive people, the apex of happiness and tranquillity is a society without differences of opinion and attitudes. But in reality, there is nothing more dangerous than this. If man is denied the right to think for himself but rather gets spoon-fed by society, then man becomes dehumanized. This is the kind of mental and moral sterility that leads to endless tyranny. It is conformism of a most destructive nature.

When all of mankind is gathered around an ideology of centralization, symbolized in a "tower" or fortress of power, then there is no longer a future for human dignity and honor. Nimrod, therefore, not only enslaved his people, he destroyed their individuality, ignored their uniqueness, and as such, turned them into meaningless numbers. His plan succeeded because it was all done under the banner of human equality and fraternity. Indeed, it takes little to convince man of his "equality" once he has been transformed into an insect. This was the tragic result of "conformity," the "uniform words" of that generation. These "words" started the long and bitter road to fascist philosophies and destructive societies.

KANT'S MISTAKE

But again, on a deeper level, it was the Kantian universal moral law, as used by Nimrod, which created the foundation for such dangerous results. This philosophy overlooks some of the most important human duties, namely, those that deal with certain relationships. Successful morality is one that understands that human beings have both stronger and less intensive relationships with their fellowmen. A father has a greater moral obligation to his children than to a stranger, as does a husband to his wife and a teacher to a student. This is extrapolated to one's extended family, community, city, and country. Without these "particularist" moral standards, mankind cannot function properly. Universal moral laws lay the foundations for disaster and undermine the very possibility of a moral society. In fact, they play right into the hands of dangerous people like Nimrod, who seek to use a so-called law of universal morality to achieve their own ends.

THE STATE AS AN OBSESSION

The state, personified in Nimrod, had now become the sole representative of all human ambition. It had became the idol of this new "world order":

> Seven ladders on the east side of the tower were used and seven on the west side. From one side they used to bring the bricks to the top, from the other, they used to descend. When a man would fall and break his neck, nobody paid any attention to him, but when a brick fell, all the men would sit down and start crying, saying: Woe to us, when will we replace this stone with another one?[21]

The state, and with it Nimrod, had become an obsession. It was no longer the welfare of man to whom the state was a means; *it was man who had become the slave of the state*, a means to the state's greater glory. The state became an end in itself. The resemblance to communism and fascist regimes becomes even more apparent.

The centrality of the tower is itself also crystal clear: Gigantic buildings, pyramids, marble monuments, and impressive squares have always been means by which the fascist state has imposed and forced its power upon its citizens. Walking around Red Square in Moscow or in other cities with overwhelming government-sponsored plazas and memorials, one starts to doubt one's own personal worth and merit. The psychological effect of these buildings and squares is to turn men into dwarfs, bowing them down to the power of the state and its officials.[22]

Reading between the lines of the story, we see how the tower represented all of Nimrod's dreams: Once assured of his absolute power over mankind, he looked "beyond." Obsessed by his own grand design and the accompanying desire for more, he now had to build a tower that would reach out to the stars—conquering space and bringing the cosmos under his feet! His "spaceship," which he would have liked to launch unto the planets (if he could have only gotten it off the ground), would have given him ultimate satisfaction. The fact that many men had to die for such an undertaking did not bother him: to die for the state and to sacrifice everything for this "great good" had, after all, become the greatest of men's privileges. True, he himself would have to be the exception to the rule, to make sure that everything followed smoothly according to plan.

SECULARISM

For the first time in human history a whole generation stood up and rebelled against God *as a matter of principle*. While earlier generations had done much evil, they understood that it was malefic and indefensible. Nimrod's wickedness, however, had brought a new ideology into being: a philosophy of extreme secularism in which God was deliberately ignored and denied. The new belief system theory saw nothing wrong in atheism and immorality; in fact, it elevated these in the form of man's new world order.

And they journeyed from the East [*Kedem*] [to the east]. Did they journey from the east to the east? Said Rabbi Elazar ben

Shimon: "It means that they journeyed away from the First One [*Kedem*] of the world." They said, "We neither need Him, nor His divinity."[23]

Mankind had brought itself to a most dangerous position. It had pushed itself to the edge of a precipice. It required a carefully measured divine response to prevent another self-imposed and unprecedented calamity.

LANGUAGE

The divine response is most unusual: "Let Us go down, so that their language will become confounded, so that they shall not understand one another's speech" (11:7).

What language did men speak at the time? As mentioned before, the Sages believed this to be the Holy Language, Hebrew. Their belief is built on the principle that Hebrew is the language through which God communicated with man. As such, it became the language in which the Torah was given. But it is also the *original* language of all men because it is the most pure of all languages.

All languages represent specific ideologies and philosophies. Cultures of nations deeply influence the nature and development of languages. Hebrew, as the language of God, denotes the intentions that God has with all His creation. It carries with it, and teaches man of, God's plan and purpose for the universe and for every creation and creature in the world. It is the language par excellence. Above all, it is a "spiritual" language, in other words, a language in which everything is seen from the perspective of its spiritual meaning. It connects everything with the ultimate Source of all being: God.[24]

As long as man somehow lived in accordance with this language and did not *deliberately* reject the word of God for an alternative life-style, Hebrew remained meaningful and alive. It was the source of man's knowledge and philosophy. But with the appearance of Nimrod and his dangerous philosophy, Hebrew slowly lost its meaning, and with that, its vitality. The Holy Language no longer identified itself with the life-style and philosophies of Nimrod's generation. In fact, the Hebrew language became a contradiction of all for which this generation stood.

The deeper meaning of the language becoming "confounded" is, therefore, not so much the result of divine intervention as it is the aftermath of men failing to understand the meaning of life and to apply its spiritual correlates. God only continued what man had started: man robbed the language of its vitality and God consequently denied man the continuous use of this language. Mankind had corrupted the language. The Hebrew word *navlah* (mixed) does not so much mean being "confounded" as it does being "dried up."[25] God tried to save "His" language from the hands of a generation that had given it a coup de grace.

THE FIRST REFUSENIK

At this moment of confusion and rebellion, a powerful personality stood up and challenged Nimrod and his generation: "At the time of the building of the tower Avraham was forty-eight years old and we do not find that he took part in this project."[26]

This became the first indication of a revolution that was to turn the world on its head. Avraham's refusal to bow down to Nimrod and his philosophy laid the foundation for a family of refuseniks, resulting in the birth of a nation of stubborn protesters and revolutionists: Israel.

Avraham understood the inherent dangers of an ideology in which God was exiled and where immorality, corruption, and sexual profligacy became the norm. While it may be possible that others may have seen this danger as well, Avraham *acted* on his belief and became actively involved in the creation of a counteroffensive that would ultimately tear down the foundations of Nimrod's empire.

But this was a task that was far from easy and fraught with all sorts of dangers. How was one man going to overthrow a mighty empire of strong, wild materialists? Avraham's critique had, therefore, to be rooted in something that would surpass all human ventures and philosophies. Realizing that there was no meaning to life unless it had an *ultimate* meaning, he started to inquire into the esoteric side of life. Before he could convince others that there was more to life than what Nimrod had to offer, he himself had to be convinced that there was. This was even more urgent because he realized that moral standards (and consequently, a better world order) had no chance of succeeding unless they were rooted in a transcendental, and therefore untouchable, entity. This led to Avraham's greatest discovery: a God of morality! This was *not* the god of Aristotle or Spinoza, who dwelt in the heavens but never touched the earth. It was a God of encounter, a personal God of personal and consequently of moral standards.

Once his penetrating mind and sensitive heart had realized the necessity of such a Being, a great transformation overtook his personality. An encounter with this newly discovered God made him realize that nobody could stand up to or destroy this belief. This "religious experience" convinced him that all men could have such an encounter and could therefore be moral. By taking on himself the task of bringing all men into a dialogue with that God, Avraham became the founder of all moral revolutions. And like him, many other great men in history, inspired by him and possessing an inner fire of truth, have stood up as lonely figures and liberated their peoples from self-destruction and oppression.

All this is reflected in the name by which Avraham became known to the world: "Avraham the *Ivri*" (the Hebrew). First, all this means that Avraham continued to speak Hebrew after everybody else had ceased to do so. This is very understandable, if we remember that Hebrew is a spiritual/moral language in which God stands in the center. Only a person of moral integrity who is prepared to hear the voice of God throughout all existence can speak a language that holds the original meaning of all creation. Consequently Avraham kept speaking Hebrew; his very personality breathed Hebrew!

Second, *Ivri* conveys the idea of "crossing a road," standing on the other side. This in itself is most symptomatic of the grandfather of the people of Israel: "The whole world stands on one side, Avraham on the other."[27] To stand for religious morality and integrity means to cross the road and to be a lonely man of faith!

His aim was to fathom the secrets of holiness, and his striving by means of admonition and moral persuasion to guide the peoples in the paths which lead mankind to spiritual and political well-being. An abiding sense of eternal will and purpose underlying human transient schemes and eternal Presence, transfusing all of life as with a hidden flame, so that love of right of man, were not only human things but also divine. (source unknown)

Avraham taught the world exactly what it did not want to hear: The most important thing in life is not what one *has* but what one *is*. He asked men to do that "which is just and right" (Genesis 18:19). This became the great mission of Avraham. And it is this that Avraham impressed upon his child Yitzchak and his grandchildren: to save the honor of mankind and to do everything to educate mankind toward its spiritual potential.

ANTI-SEMITISM

Such an undertaking could not fail to create problems. Once Avraham had launched his new mission, he encountered tremendous opposition. Nimrod, seeing him as a major challenge, could not think of anything else but to silence this disturbing and "offensive" voice. This reaction started a long and barbarous road of anti-Semitism. While it must be argued that anti-Semitism does not seem to be rooted in any logic or reason, the rejection of the Jewish moral view is no doubt one of its best advocates.

Nimrod, like all anti-Semites, realized that silencing the power of Avraham's message was out of the question. Only the physical destruction of the Jew would silence this voice. With this realization, Nimrod became the inventor of the "ideology" of concentration camps and gas chambers. He then confronted Avraham with two options: either bow down to him and live or doggedly hold on to the Abrahamic God and face the first gas chamber in the form of a fiery furnace.[28] Hatred is rooted in fear and is the coward's reaction to the feeling of being threatened.

Avraham's response to this threat was even more extreme: better to die for the truth than to live in a world of falsehood. This defiant act laid the foundation for all Jewish refusal to compromise or renounce the monotheistic truth. Avraham's escape from this first concentration camp cannot simply be written off as a miracle. As the only Jew, and therefore *the* Jew, he *had* to survive. This was the promise made to Avraham and his descendants—that the people of Israel would never die. It was a clear warning to all anti-Semites that their dream to silence the voice of morality would never be realized.

At the end of this episode, Avraham quietly went his way and slowly forged a religious, moral movement: "And Avram took Sarai his wife and Lot his brother's son and all their substance that they had gathered and the souls they had gotten at Charan" (Genesis 12:5). According to Rashi,[29] "The text indicates that Avraham had brought them under the wings of the Divine Presence. Avraham proselytized the men and Sara proselytized the women."

Avraham, his family, and all those who surrounded him became "a living protest against superstition and religious materialism" (Ernest Renan). And so he began to build a nation that was to become the guilty conscience of the world. "The Jews gave the world no peace, they bar slumber, they teach the world to be discontented and restless as long as the world has no God" (Jacques Maritain).

As such, the Jew became an embarrassment to the world. Like Avraham, Jews started to irritate the world. Consequently, they became the scapegoat for all national and social hysteria. But Avraham, knowing his task, pressed on with his mission to form the nation that was prepared to pay the ultimate price in order to save mankind from all antireligious and immoral ideologies: the Sanctification of God's Name (*Kiddush Ha-Shem*). Infusing mankind with the notion of *kedushah* (holiness), Avraham called for a "kingdom of priests, charged with the task to instruct and teach the whole of mankind, in order that they may call upon the name of God and serve Him with one consent."[30]

Nothing is therefore more manifest than the fact that the chosenness of the Jew has absolutely nothing in common with the racist *Herrenvolk* philosophy of the Nazis or that of any other nation. While the Nazis believed that they, as a superior nation, had *to be served* by the rest of mankind, the Jews understood themselves *to be the servants of mankind*.[31]

The Jewish ideal, therefore, is not a monopoly on God or ethics but rather a sharing and promoting of these very ideas. The ultimate purpose of the chosenness of the Jews is the establishment of a *chosen mankind*, in which Jews are no longer needed.

THE LAND OF ISRAEL

Within this present framework we may also understand the purpose of the Land of Israel. The Jewish settlement in the Land of Israel is not a goal in itself but only a means to bring the message of Avraham to the world. It should become a spiritual center of the people of Israel, not its purpose! Israel is to be a power source from which all Jews draw their spiritual energy. From this standpoint, we can understand the purpose of the different aspects of the *galut* (exile) phenomenon. Although *galut* is primarily the result of a national deviation from the ways of the Torah (Leviticus 26:33), it has another purpose as well: *galut* gave Jews the opportunity to make an important contribution to the non-Jewish world. The presence of Jews within gentile societies exerted a positive influence on the world community at large. Many ethi-

cal ideas, as taught by the Jewish tradition, gave birth to great
social changes. These considerations are, however, second-
ary when compared to Jewish potential within the Land of
Israel. Only in Israel does the possibility exist for Jews to
create a model state—a highly advanced society in which
economics, science, culture, and even its defense forces are
elevated and imbued with an ethical religious character. This
is the meaning of Israel becoming *a light to the nations*:[32]

> Relate among the nations His honor, among all the peoples
> His wonders. Say among the nations: The lord reigns. (Psalm
> 96:3, 10)

While all Jews should be inhabitants of the Land, some,
specially trained for the task, should be sent for short periods
at a time to different countries of the world so as to share with
them some of the more universal aspects of Judaism. Care
should be taken so as not to create a definite and specific Jewish
community outside the borders of Israel. It should be argued
that in the framework of Jewish statehood and self-reliance,
Jews would, on the whole, feel more secure, and therefore more
in touch with their roots, enabling them to inspire the world
to ever greater heights and hasten the final Redemption.

OPTING IN AND OUT

According to earlier observations in this chapter, a Jew is a
moral protester who understands his task as bringing the
great ethical teachings of pure monotheism to the world. His
is a most difficult road to travel, with many obstacles. It is a
road that brings with it much annoyance and unpopularity,
a task that requires constant self-discipline, personal integ-

rity, and a lot of nerve. The stakes are high and the encounter with virulent anti-Semitism is ever near.

The situation raises a host of questions: Why does the Jewish tradition allow a non-Jew to "opt in" to the Jewish faith but never allows a Jew to "opt out"?

Why does the *halachah* (Jewish law) determine that all human beings born of a Jewish mother are to be Jewish? Would it not have been more logical to leave it up to the individuals—those who wish to take this difficult task upon themselves are Jews and those who do not are not?

Why should human beings be forced to belong to a particular ideology when they themselves do not subscribe to that very ideology? Why make people members of a nation whose purpose is to be a "light to the nations" when they themselves do not see that light? Is this not blatantly unjustified? What does this mean for the millions of Jews who feel no longer affiliated with the message of Judaism? Why continue to call them Jews just because they happen to be born of a Jewish mother?

Looking into the history of the Jews over the last few hundred years, one may wonder what the reason could be for holding on to so many who rejected everything Jewish and sometimes even vehemently opposed their Jewishness. Some declared themselves to be atheists and others members or even leaders of other religions.[33]

How long can one remain a member of a club when one violates all its rules?

ROOT EXPERIENCES

The answer to this barrage of questions requires a quick rerun of Jewish history. When Avraham embarked on his great mission to save the world, he started by bringing in a small amount of people and thereby forging a special nation. This process did not come to an end until Jews stood, many hundreds of years later, at Sinai. Only there, through the receiving of the Torah and the *mitzvot* (commandments), did the Jews become the official Israelite nation. The long period preceding this event was the duration in which "the Jew was in the making," a period in which the unique Jewish character was being molded.

It was due to a great amount of most unusual experiences that Jews became what they had to become. We shall call these experiences "root experiences." These experiences became deeply implanted in the collective consciousness and ethos of the people of Israel, never to be extirpated. Through trials, tribulations, and moments of great exaltation, a specific psyche with specific dispositions was being molded.

The long and difficult wanderings of the earlier Hebrews, with their trials, sufferings, and nearly endless exiles, left a deep imprint on their souls. The frequent divine encounters and their protest marches through their early history forged an inner spiritual energy of incredible strength. The battle for justice and morality and the continuous cultivation of monotheism through waging war with worldwide polytheism created a spiritual stubbornness that was never to disappear. Avraham's readiness to sacrifice his son, Yitzchak, was of such far-reaching consequences that it became the very life force of all Jews. The troubles of Jacob with his brother Esav and uncle Laban, his encounter with the angel, and his bitter experience with his sons in their expulsion of their own brother, Joseph, embedded themselves into the very hearts of all Jews. The crushing experience of Egypt, the psychological shock of the ten plagues, and the traumatic exodus had a cathartic effect on all coming generations. The miraculous survival for forty years in the desert on their way to the Holy Land, the pillar of fire, and the cloud of glory guiding their way must have left an indelible impression upon the hearts and souls of millions of Jews and their children. Living in the presence of personalities like Moshe, Aharon, Miriam, and many others was beyond undoing. While the journey through the Red Sea must have brought jubilation to the hearts of all Jews, the totally unprecedented revelation at Sinai became the grandest moment in Jewish history. It caused universal upheaval and became *the* Jewish experience, branding itself on all Jewish hearts for all time.

A different type of human being emerged, rooted in a mysterious metaphysical history. Through an endless amount of these most unusual "root experiences," Jews became a people with an inborn aptitude and calling for a higher spiritual mission. Their very personalities became identified with these experiences, and consequently, with this new task. They became the natural carriers of ethical monotheism. It became the air they breathed. For this reason it was, and is, no longer possible for them to "opt out." Trying to undo or deny these root experiences would be like somebody trying to get out of his own skin. Ignoring their task as the educators of the world would be an act of severe self-abnegation with disastrous consequences. There *was* and *is* no way back anymore. To "opt out" became, and is, a contradiction in terms.

This is the rationale behind the law that states that all human beings born of a Jewish mother are to be seen as Jews. No other option was open to *halachah*! The mother as the physical *and* spiritual incubator of the child to be born steeps it into four thousand years of Jewish experience. The child is soaked in the collective Jewish experience of spiritual mission and dedication.

When Jews deny or ignore their mission in this world,

they are, according to *halachah*, guilty of self-deception. It is unnatural for them not to live in conformity with their spiritual task.[34]

Opting out no longer belongs to the eventualities. It is too late.

A Jew who lives up to his historical task, as a world-transforming being, may indeed be an alien creature in the history of man, but a Jew who tries to free himself of this task and attempts to be like the rest of mankind becomes even more alien.

613 AND 7

Jews are required to live by the 613 *mitzvot* (commandments).[35] They are also asked to become a "light to the nations," an example to the world. From this it would follow that Jews should actively inspire the rest of the world to commit themselves to the 613 commandments. It is, therefore, most peculiar that this is far from the truth! If gentiles came and told the Jews that they had heard of their great message and that they would have to keep all these commandments themselves, the Jews would discourage them from doing so! Only Jews should keep all these commandments. Non-Jews have no obligation to convert and therefore no moral obligation to keep *Shabbat*, the dietary laws, and many more laws mentioned in the Torah. This is startling: one inspires a non-Jew to hear the voice of monotheism and its implications, only to tell him afterward that there is no need to yield to its demands!

The answer to this puzzle is as follows: "To bring down from heaven the everlasting fire, which needs to illumine the entire world and to become the religious source, spring and fountain from which all the rest of the peoples will draw their beliefs and religions"[36] is not an easy task.

Like Avraham, all Jews are a lonely people. They are small in number and constantly being beaten. And just like the first Jew, they have to stand up against a mighty world that is hostile to their message. How could such a mission have any chance to succeed?

It is for this very reason that the 613 *mitzvot* become of crucial importance. For Jews to become the great transformers of a misguided world, they are themselves in need of constant inspiration. Since their numbers are totally out of proportion to their task, there must be a way of "compensating" for this great drawback. This was achieved by offsetting quantity with quality.

Together with their collective root experiences, the Jews were to be inspired and constantly reminded of their exalted task. The commandments, penetrating into every aspect of life, kept Jews on their toes. Israel was in need of more than a basic code of morals. This need was met with the acceptance of the Torah at Sinai. The purpose of the Covenant within the Torah was to guide the Jew, never allowing him to lose sight of his lofty task despite the vicissitudes of his troubled existence.

For the world to become civilized in the spiritual sense, there is no need for all men to keep the 613 commandments. God gave the first man and his spouse a body of wide-ranging religious and ethical constitution, known as the seven laws of Noach.[37] These seven laws comprise hundreds of ethical directives. Many found their way into the secular legal system, for example, international law and the general moral standards of Western society.[38]

No doubt, Judaism accepts the idea of universality, like the one Kant espouses, but not at the expense of particularistic covenants. The Covenant that God created with Noach is universal, since it is built on the principle of all men being created in the image of God, whereas the Covenant with Avraham, which was later intensified at Sinai, is a particular "pact," creating a special bond between all Jews and sharing a collective responsibility toward the rest of the world.

As mentioned earlier, this collective responsibility among Jews expresses itself in numerous laws, such as an "agreement" not to charge interest, special care for the property of others, and so forth, to the exclusion of non-Jews (even though one is definitely encouraged to treat non-Jews alike). This is similar to a "brotherhood," where its constituents have agreed to carry greater responsibility for each other than what basic morality would require.

It should be argued that it is exactly this particularity that is the cornerstone for a real and healthy moral society. How does one treat the stranger, the one who is *not* one's brother? To care for one's brother goes without saying; to care for the stranger is a completely different matter. In the Torah and rabbinical tradition, we find numerous laws that demand an ethical relationship with the non-Jew, "because you were yourselves strangers in the land of Egypt" (Exodus 22:20; 23:9). This command is mentioned thirty-six times in the Torah![39]

There is a universal Covenant that sets the minimum conditions for a peaceful world, but beyond that there lies the principle of the intrinsic plurality of man, which expresses itself in different faith communities with particular relationships existing among members of those communities.

The idea of election necessarily implies exclusiveness. To go one's own way means to reject the way of others. When one stands alone and in opposition to all others, one must create one's own life: "Lo, the people that dwells alone and does not reckon itself among the nations" (Numbers 23:9).

Whenever exclusiveness is lacking, there follows, as history demonstrates, syncretism. However, the exclusiveness of the Jewish People is of a most particular kind, where *national exclusiveness is transformed into ethical exclusiveness.* To abandon national exclusiveness is to destroy ethical exclusiveness. Destroy the people and you destroy their heritage and their mission. Although Jews may give the impression of being a narrow, nationalistic, self-centered people, they are, in fact, universalistic in outlook.

Judaism, unlike the heritages of other nations, is not embodied in any book, not even in the Torah. It is found in a living reality, in its way of life, which was built on the highest ideals known to man. It is concrete actions and not abstract ideas that will transform mankind into a chosen humanity. There needs to be an affirmation of a living God who operates within life and history, God who meets man in the here and now.[40]

4

On the Law of the
Mamzer—Fair or Holy?

"A *mamzer* shall not enter in the congregation of the Lord." (Deuteronomy 23:3)

cardinal principle of Jewish law is that it not only must be equitable but it also must be manifestly seen as being fair. There is one law that, on the face of it, breaches both these principles.

The *halachah* states that a *mamzer* is prevented from marrying a fellow Jew or Jewess. Only fellow *mamzerim* or proselytes are potential candidates as this person's partner in life.[1] According to rabbinic definition, a *mamzer* is a child born from a couple whose sexual relationship is forbidden according to the Torah and punishable by *karet,* or death.[2] Because of this, a marriage between them is void; thus, for example, the issue of a union between brother and sister or between a woman validly married to another at the time and a man is a *mamzer.*[3]

While recognizing the inherent wrong in these liaisons and the social damage caused thereby, one may be forgiven for wondering how the Torah could introduce a law so apparently unjustifiable and inhumane: that a child pay the price for the misdeeds of the parents. This would appear, in fact, to contradict another basic Torah principle, namely, that

77

each person is responsible for his or her own actions, or for
those of a neighbor when the person is in a position to prevent transgression. However, in this case the unborn child
is already condemned for life, before he or she could do anything right or wrong!

Logically, there seems to be no way to justify this biblical
ruling, and therefore, one may perhaps argue that it should
be seen as purely theoretical. This, for example, is the case with
the law concerning the *ben sorer u'more*, the rebellious son
(Deuteronomy 21:18-21). The Sages declared that the conditions for passing a death sentence in such a case were so strin-
gent and remote that they could never be met; rather, the case
was only stated to increase the reward for those who study
this verse as part of the *mitzvah* of Talmud Torah.[4]

Why, then, do the Rabbis, or for that matter the Oral
Tradition, not declare the law of the *mamzer* to be similarly
theoretical, as in the case of the *ben sorer u'more*? This might
be the best solution; anything else would be impossible. To
ignore the law or to see it as an actual error created by primitive men, as Spinoza and others would declare, is obviously
not an option for the believing Jew, since Jewish tradition sees
every word of the Torah as being beyond reproach. The law
of the Torah is of divine origin and cannot be lightly cast aside.

We are thus confronted with an unusual situation, for
we are forced to admit that this embarrassing and apparently
unjustifiable law is part of our divine heritage! This is more
than a paradox; it is acutely painful.

At this point, the reader may be wondering how the
author dares to make such a controversial statement about
a law found within the Torah. However, careful examination
will show that in fact he has the full weight of Jewish tradition behind him.

GOD VERSUS GOD

We read in Ecclesiastes (4:1) the following: "So I returned and considered all the oppressions that are done under the sun, and behold the tears of such as were oppressed. And they had no comforter, and on the side of their oppressors there was power, but they had no comforter."

The Midrash comments:[5]

"Behold the tears of the oppressed"—their fathers sinned, but what has this to do with these insulted ones? The father of this one went to a woman forbidden to him, but how did the child sin, and why does it concern him? "They have no comforter . . . but in the hands of the oppressors there is power"—these are the hands of the Great Sanhedrin,[6] which moved against them with the authority of the Torah and removed them from the community, because it is written: "A *mamzer* shall not enter in the congregation of the Eternal One."

"And there is none to comfort them"—therefore says the Holy One, Blessed be He: "It is upon Me to comfort them. . . . " As Zechariah (4:1) prophesied: "Behold I see them all like pure gold."

This midrash reflects an inherent paradox, which is symptomatic of traditional Jewish thought. It is a case of God versus God: God the Oppressor and God the Comforter. The same God who is the Author of, "A *mamzer* shall not enter in the congregation of the Eternal One" is also the God who is the Great Comforter: "Behold I see them all like pure gold."

THE PROBLEM OF EVIL

The phenomenon of "God versus God" is most clearly expressed in the problem of good and evil: God is the Creator of both of them.

> Creating light, forming darkness making peace and creating evil I, the Lord, do all these things. (Isaiah 45:6-7)

Immediately the age-old question comes to mind, Why does God, the merciful Creator of the world, need to create evil? Could He not have created a world entirely without evil? The answer is clearly no!

The world, after all, has a purpose, a raison d'être.

John Hick, professor of Philosophy at the University of Birmingham, calls the world "a soul-making place," a place where people can spiritually grow, overcome obstacles, and become more "soullike." For our purposes, and more in line with Jewish thought, we would like to adapt Hick's phraseology and call it a *tzaddik*-making place, namely, a place where righteous people can come into being. Since this world needs to be an arena for *tzaddik*-making, it must by definition consist of good and evil, argues Hick and many others.

Here Hick introduces his "counterfactual hypothesis":

> Suppose that, contrary to fact, this world were a paradise from which all possibility of pain and suffering were excluded. The consequences would be very far-reaching. For example, no one could ever injure anyone else, the murderer's knife would turn to paper or the bullets to thin air, the bank safe, robbed of a million dollars, would miraculously become filled with another million dollars; fraud,

deceit, conspiracy, and treason would somehow leave the fabric of society undamaged. No one would ever be injured by accident: the mountain climber, steeplejack, or a playing child falling from a height would float unharmed to the ground, the reckless driver would never meet with disaster. In a hedonistic paradise there would be no wrong actions nor therefore any right actions in distinction from wrong. Courage and fortitude would have no point in an environment in which there is, by definition, no danger or difficulty. Generosity, kindness, the agape aspect of love, prudence unselfishness, and other ethical notions that presuppose life in an objective environment could not even be formed. Consequently, such a world, however well it might promote pleasure, would be very ill adapted for the moral qualities of human personality. In relation to this purpose it might well be the worst of all possible worlds![7]

It all comes down to one principle: For man to reach ethical good, he will need to pay a price by learning to cope with evil.

This is the divine dilemma: If God had created a perfect world from the outset, it would have been one of unmitigated evil. Since He wanted a world where evil would no longer exist, He was obliged to create one with evil! What this means in practice is that for the world to exist, certain fundamental conditions must be fulfilled. This is not an apology, it is a conditio sine qua non. To say that this world should be without evil is to say that the world should not exist.

Just as there can be no meaning in speaking about light without a concomitant darkness, neither can one speak about good without evil, sympathy without aversion, humility without arrogance, honesty without falsehood, *kedushah* (holiness) without *tuma'h* (impurity).

Now, let us ask, Is evil fair? Are injustice, pain, war, and illness fair? From the human perspective, the answer must be definitely no! But if we ask the question, "Are these necessary entities without which the world cannot exist?" The answer must be a resounding yes! They are the collateral we have to pay if we want to achieve and experience good health, peace, and justice.

KEDUSHAH (HOLINESS)

Now all this seems to be far removed from the law of mamzerut. The same questions may, however, be asked in this case. Is it fair? Most definitely not! It is as unfair as pain, war, and illness. This is exactly what the earlier quoted midrash says: a law stating that a child must pay the price for the transgressions of his or her parents cannot be anything else but unfair, and as such, unjustifiable.

What, then, is the divine imperative underlying the institution? Why indeed does it find a place in the Torah at all? The answer is the same as with good and evil. It is a necessary counterforce for the creation of a greater good, as explained by the counterfactual hypothesis. This time, however, it is not the creation of some sort of negative force to allow a positive one to come into realization (as in the case of good and evil) but the creation of a prohibition so as to achieve the highest level of biblical imperative: *kedushah*, holiness.

The Jewish People is called upon to become an *Am Kadosh* (a Holy Nation) and a *Mamlechet Kohanim* (Kingdom of Priests). The Jewish People is asked to achieve a high level of *kedushah*, not for its own sake but for the sake of mankind: a light unto the nations! This, however, cannot be achieved without a counterforce.

SEXUALITY

There is one litmus test by which a nation's *kedushah* can be measured. This is the most basic element of the human personality and its expression: sexuality. Sexuality is one of the most powerful human passions and, as experience has constantly shown, the breaking point of civilization. Whole empires have fallen apart because of the idolization of sex; crimes have been committed and even wars begun because of this most powerful urge.

It is no coincidence that the *brit milah*, the circumcision, is chosen as the great sign of the Jewish Covenant with God. The attitude toward, and the handling of, sexual passion is the ultimate test. It is the best yardstick of man's commitment to *kedushah* and morality. This is perhaps the very reason the Bible contains so many laws concerning sexuality. Judaism shuns the abolition or the denial of the sexual urge. It abhors the extreme idea of human sexuality being an aberration, a concession to sinful man. It does not countenance the idea of absolute self-denial and suppression. Rather, it calls for the careful handling and sublimation of this most important and God-given urge.

To make sure that the Jewish People achieve the greatest possible *kedushah* in the world, a counterforce had to be created. This is the underlying purpose of the law of the *mamzer*. Nothing could make it more evident to the Jew how careful he needs to be in dealing with matters of sexuality and *kedushah* than this very institution. By making the child pay for the transgression of the most severe of all sexual prohibitions (adultery), the Torah created a counterforce so far-reaching and so "unjustified" that it would, once and for all, create the highest of all goodnesses: *kedushah*. To achieve that goal, the Torah touched the Jew at his most sensitive spot: his child. Many a Jew might perhaps be prepared to transgress the severest of laws, and carry the consequences personally, but would not do so with the knowledge that his child will pay the price.

It is not just the *mamzer* law, or the individual involved, that is at the heart of the matter. What is at the bottom of it is that through this law the Jewish People would become aware of their highest goals and that human sexuality, the greatest of all passions, can and must be sanctified. Only then can one speak of a Holy Nation and of a Chosen People. Through this law, the existence of a proper family life, the foundation of the Jewish nation, becomes a reality. The *mamzer* law, then, hovers over the Jew's whole life as a powerful force to guarantee the survival of the Jewish People and the fulfillment of its great mission toward the world community: to be a world-transforming people.

In this sense we may say that the *mamzer* law guaranteed the survival of the Jewish nation and gave it a vitality not observed among other peoples.

AKEIDAT YITZCHAK

Throughout history the Jew has had to sacrifice his child. This was a powerful means through which he would never forget his destination and his raison d'être.

His child was, and is, his guarantee for this ongoing commitment. It was not without reason that the greatest of all Jews, Avraham, underwent the supreme test of giving up his child to show his total commitment to his God and the Jewish mission. His faith, and his survival through that test, became the supreme example and the paradigm for the future of the Jewish People. Without that unprecedented experi-

ence, no Chosen People would have emerged and no Torah
would have been given.

But was the *akeidat Yitzchak* (the sacrifice of Isaac) fair?
Within the scope of the private life of Avraham, and even
more so of Yitzchak, it was uncalled for! It was not even
Yitzchak's trial. He was the victim of someone else's test!
If, however, we ask whether this trial was a necessity in
order to forge the links in creating an *Am Kadosh* and a
Mamlechet Kohanim, then the answer must be an unquali-
fied yes.

Everything must be subsumed by the survival and the
great task of the Jewish People. This is the purpose of Israel's
ultimate sacrifice. This is the paradox of all Jewish religious
thought.

FAIRNESS

What becomes clear is this: fairness is not the ultimate criterion in Jewish law or thought. It is not an ultimate standard.
"Derache'ha darchei noam" (Your ways are ways of pleasant-
ness) (Proverbs 3:17-18) expressed a rule much used by the
Talmud to determine the more pleasant approach of the
halachah toward otherwise unpleasant circumstances, but
this *not* an absolute value.[8] It can be overshadowed by an even
higher imperative: *kedushah* (holiness) and the survival and
mission of the Jewish People. Fairness is only of value if it is
not an obstacle to the achievement of *kedushah*.

In the great scheme of Jewish history, the law regarding *mamzerut* has been an absolute essential and crucial element in the unfolding of God's purpose for mankind and
the world. But God is also the Comforter. When the Messianic Era starts and Israel has reached its ultimate goal, then
the world will be transformed by the spiritual ideals of the

Torah and the *mamzer* law will have no further purpose. This, then, is the meaning of the talmudic statement, "*Mamzerim* are to be purified in the Messianic Age."[9]

As long as these days have not arrived, the *mamzer* law functions as one of the most effective ways of achieving this very goal.

5

On Particularism
and Universalism

articularism (the belief that God chose the Jewish People to be His distinctive people), universalism, and the equality of men are the pillars on which Judaism stands.[1] The last two are not the outcome of some evolutionary process that started with a primitive belief in a tribal God and later developed into the great message of universal monotheism, but rather they are part and parcel of the Jewish biblical worldview from its very inception.

In fact, particularism, being the central pillar of Judaism, is a conduit through which universalism and equality flow. Were it not for particularism, social justice, human rights, and freedom of speech and assembly would have no real influence on human ethics. They would have remained as abstract concepts, without ever touching earth.

PARTICULARISM AND UNIVERSALISM

In any discussion concerning Israel's exclusiveness, the following has to be understood: All biblical references to the

"Chosen People" are made in a universalistic context. The election of Israel is only possible within a universalistic framework:

> Now, therefore, if you will obey My voice indeed, and keep My covenant, then you shall be a peculiar treasure unto Me, above all people: *For all the earth is Mine.* (Exodus 19:15) (italics added)

> Why do you say O Jacob, and speak O Israel, my way is hid from the Lord, and my judgment is passed over from my God, do you not know, have you not heard, that the everlasting God, the Lord, the Creator of *the ends of the earth* fainteth not, neither is weary? There is no searching of His understanding. (Isaiah 40:27-28) (italics added)

> Thus says God the Lord, *He spread the heavens,* and stretched them forth, He spread forth the earth and that which comes out of it. He that gives bread unto the people upon it, *and spirit to them that walk therein,* I, the Lord have called the righteous men, and have taken hold of your land, and kept them and set you for a covenant of the people *for a light to the nations,* to open the blind eyes. To bring out the prisoners from the dungeon and them that sit in darkness out of the prison-house. (Isaiah 42:5-7) (italics added)

These verses make an extremely important point: the Bible does not see ethics and religious values as abstract propositions only to be apprehended intellectually or as some esoteric wisdom to be received through some kind of religious mysticism.

The ethical messages of the Bible are founded on faith enacted in history and not to be experienced, understood, or communicated outside their historical reality. They are not timeless statements, as is the case in Buddhism, regarding the source of human misery and the way to liberation. The biblical and, therefore, the Jewish weltanschauung is one that is redemptive in purpose—a kind of *Heilsgeschichte*, redemptive history—a history of here and now, in which the ultimate goal, the Messianic Era, is not "beyond" but "within" the framework of human day-to-day existence.

It is *real* history in the sense that it captures *das Ding an sich*—the absolute thing that turns history into a journey from creation to redemption. Physical and spiritual *ge'ulah* (redemption) can only be achieved through a divine plan based on justice and righteousness. The history of the Jewish People points to the real history of all mankind. This is the meaning of, "When the Most High gave the nations their inheritance; when He separated the sons of Adam, he set the boundaries of nations, according to the number of the children of Israel" (Deuteronomy 32:8).

All nations find their history in the account of biblical historical narrative because "the fear of God" is the key to the unfolding of all historical reality. The Western mind may balk at the notion of a universal God acting through the particularities of history, but that is only true because it fails to understand the essential message of all biblical thought: universal ideas are impersonal and therefore inconsequential. Salvation, however, is through a personal relationship and actions. Truly personal relationships are never universal; they are always concrete and particular. And while an idea or a doctrine may be made available to all men universally throughout time, it can only be carried by the individual or a group of human beings in the here and now. This has been called the "Abrahamic postulate," the affirmation of a living God, operating through life and history, who meets man in a personal encounter.

Redemptive history means the unfolding of a redemptive message, from the particular to the universal.

CHOSEN MANKIND

God's choice of Israel was, therefore, not for the sake of Israel but for the sake of mankind: *From a chosen people to a chosen mankind*. With this achieved, Israel's *Heilsgeschichte* would come to an end. In that sense, Israel's historical role is to call itself out of existence.[2]

One may ask, "Why Israel?" Many suggestions have been put forward. Abraham Geiger, the German reform leader, claimed that Jews have a special genius for religion; Alfred Whitehead saw them as the most able race in existence.[3] Others saw Israel as a people of moral protesters. Whatever the truth may be, the Bible itself makes it very clear that the choice of Israel was reciprocal: Israel chose God, and *therefore,* God chose Israel:

> Thou has avouched the Lord this day to be your God, and to walk in His ways, and keep His statues, and His commandments, and His judgments and to hearken unto His voice, and the Lord has avouched you this day to be His peculiar people, as He promised you, and that you should keep His commandments. (Deuteronomy 26:17-18)

> And Joshua said unto the people: "you are witnesses against yourselves that you have chosen you the Lord to serve Him"; and they said: "we are witnesses." (Joshua 24:22).

THE NATION OF ISRAEL

Maimonides, in his famous *Codex of Jewish Law*, writes that Avraham recognized his Master when he was forty years old, broke the idols of those days, and influenced tens of thousands of people to believe in God and follow His moral instruction.[4] This mission he passed on to his children and grandchildren, and so Israel became a source of righteousness and justice in a world that worshiped wealth and lust. Israel has had, since that day, an unprecedented influence on the world. Never did a nation with so few people have such an overwhelming effect on the hearts and minds of all men.

Lyman Abbot wrote:

> We gentiles owe our life to Israel. It is Israel who has brought us the message that God is One, and that God is a just and righteous God, and demands righteousness of His children, and demands nothing else. It is Israel that has brought us the message that God is our Father. It is Israel who brought us the divine law, has laid the foundation of liberty. It is Israel who had the first free institution the world ever saw. It is Israel who has brought us our Bible, our prophets, our apostles. When sometimes our own unchristian prejudices flame out against the Jewish people, let us remember that all that we have and all that we owe, under God, is due to what Judaism has given us.[5]

It becomes extremely evident that the doctrine of the Chosen People has nothing in common with the idea of *Herrenvolk*. On the contrary, it stands for a nation dedicated to the service of others. The constant castigation of their people by the prophets, their repeated demands that the people live up to their vocation, in which they are failing lamentably, and their frequent warnings against incurring divine displeasure are hardly ideas that one could associate with divine favoritism.[6] Didn't somebody once say that the Bible is an anti-Semitic book?[7]

One is reminded of Pascal's famous remark: "And to this Book that relates so many evil things of them, they cling with their whole heart, and defend it at the cost of their lives. *This is unparalleled sincerity*"[8] (italics added).

Neither has the doctrine any affinity with such notions as that of Aryan racial superiority. Jewish particularism is never exclusive. Anyone can become a Jew by embracing the Jewish faith. Even a member of Amalek, the archenemy of Israel, "whose memory should be blotted out" (Deuteronomy 35:17), could become a member of the Jewish nation were he or she to opt seriously for the laws and ethics of Judaism.[9] Do not the Messiah and King David descend from a Moabite woman called Ruth?

REPLACEMENT THEOLOGY

Theologians who believe that the Church (or any other faith community) has taken the place of Israel as God's chosen people are contradicted by sober historical facts:

1. Israel's miraculous survival for four thousand years.
2. Its remarkable contribution to civilization and religion.
3. Its unprecedented return to its homeland after two thousand years.

Israel's constant violation of all rules of natural survival, as evidenced by outliving six empires, holocausts, inquisitions, and pogroms and by living most of the time without a homeland or army, has not only shocked historians but has also remained totally unexplained. Only a special divine protection may account for this historical phenomenon.

Israel has proportionally generated more social revolutions and religious teachings than any other nation. Its contribution to science, psychology, and other forms of human knowledge has astonished more than just a few people. Its remarkable role in human history to this very day makes one wonder if God actually did remove His "special" love from this people, even after the Holocaust.

The "replacement" theology of certain Christian theologians, however, received its final blow with the return of Israel to its homeland. Its unprecedented "reappearance" into history, three years after the whole world believed it had witnessed Israel's final defeat, has given those theologians a most difficult reality to deal with: God's *eternal* devotion to the People of Israel.[10]

Both implicit and explicit, the ethics of Judaism are the beliefs in the fatherhood of God and the brotherhood of man. Thus Malachi (2:10) cried out, "Have we not all one Father, hath not One God created us?" This is the fatherhood principle. But in the same breath the Prophet continues: "Why do we deal treacherously every man against his brother?" This is the brotherhood principle. The fatherhood and brotherhood principles are inseparable: if we have the same Father, then we are brothers.

GOD'S IMAGE

The most clear expression of the fatherhood of God and the brotherhood of man is the biblical statement that all men are created in the image of God. This is not a latter invention of prophetic theology but the first statement the Bible ever made about man. The Sages of Israel did not tire of delivering homilies giving figurative expression to the oneness of the human family. The following statement made by the Mishnah (*Sanhedrin* 37a) reveals this universal message:

Only one single man was created in the world, to teach that, if any man had caused a single soul to perish, Scripture imputes it to him as though he had caused a whole world to perish; and if any man saves a single soul, Scripture imputes it to him as though he has saved a whole world. Again, but a single man was created for the sake of peace among mankind, that none should say to his fellow, "My father was greater than your father"; also that the heretics should not say, "There are many ruling powers in heaven." Again, but a single man was created to proclaim the greatness of God, for man stamps many coins with one die, and they are all like to one another; but God has stamped every man with the die of the first man, yet no one of them is like his fellow. Therefore every one must say, "For my sake was the world created."

The Talmud also raises the question of why man was created as a solitary human being, which the Talmud answers, "So that it might not be said that some races are better than others."[11]

Consider statements like: "I call heaven and earth to witness that whether a person be Jew or gentile, man or woman, manservant or maidservant, according to his acts, does the divine spirit rest upon him?"[12] "If a man wishes to become a priest, he cannot, why? Because his father was not a priest or levite. But if a man wants to be righteous, he can, also a gentile. Righteousness is not a matter of family. It is those 'who fear the Lord,' not the house of those who fear the Lord, that the psalmist [Psalm 115:11] calls on to bless the Lord. The righteous are not a hereditary house but men who, of their own volition, offered themselves and loved God; therefore God loves them."[13]

"How do we know then when a non-Jew who occupies himself with the Torah is like a high priest? For it is written in Leviticus 18:5: 'And you shall guard My laws and My social laws, which if a man do, he shall live thereby'—not Priest, Levite, or Israelite, but *man*. Thus, you learn that a non-Jew who engages in Torah is like a high priest."[14]

NON-JEWS AND THE OBLIGATION TO HONOR PARENTS

Most remarkable is the statement that Jews should learn from gentiles to honor one's parents:[15]

Rabbi Eliezer was asked: How far does the honor of parents extend? Said he: "Go forth and see what a certain non-Jew, Dama, son of Nethinah by name, did in Ashkelon." The Sages sought jewels for the ephod [breastplate for the high priest] at a profit of six hundred thousand golden denari . . . but as the key was lying under his father's pillow, he did not trouble him. The following year the Holy One, Blessed be He, gave him his reward: A red heifer[16] was born to him in his herd. When the Sages of Israel went to him [to buy it] he said to them: "I know you, that even if I asked you for all the money in the world you would pay me, but I ask you only the money I lost through my father's honor."

SANCTIFYING GOD'S NAME

The injunctions in the Bible relating to the treatment of a brother were *not* considered as being directed only to the treatment of Israelites but were considered directed to all mankind. This point is made by the midrash informing us about the following incident:[17]

Simon Ben Shatah was occupied with preparing flax. His
disciples said to him, "Rabbi, desist. We will buy you an ass,
and you will not have to work so hard." They went and
bought an ass from an Arab, and a pearl was found on it,
whereupon they came to him and said: "From now on you
need not work anymore." "Why?" he asked. They said, "We
bought you an ass from an Arab, and a pearl was found on
it." He said to them, "Does its owner know of that?" They
answered, "No." He said to them, "Go and give the pearl back
to him." "But," they argued, "did not Rabbi Huna, in the name
of Rav, say all the world agrees that if you find something
that belongs to a heathen, you may keep it?" Their teacher
said, "Do you think that Simon ben Shatah is a barbarian?
He would prefer to hear the Arab say, 'Blessed be the God
of the Jews,' than possess all the riches of the world. . . . It is
written, 'Thou shall not oppress thy neighbor.' Now your
neighbor is as your brother, and your brother is as your
neighbor. Hence you learn that to rob a gentile is robbery."

In another source we read:[18] In a city where there are
both Jews and gentiles, the collector of alms collects both
from Jews and gentiles, feeds the poor of both, buries both,
comfort the mourners whether they be Jews or gentiles, and
restores the last goods of both.

The Torah starts the Creation of Man not with the birth
of Abraham but with the creation of Adam and Eve. The Sages
stated that Adam was made from the dust gathered by God
from the four corners of the earth, so that no people could
say that man was made from the dust gathered only in their
own corner of the world.[19]

Whenever one turns to later Jewish sources, the fatherhood of God and the equality and brotherhood of man are
recurring themes. At the Passover *seder* a drop of wine is to
be spilled from the cup at the mention of each of the ten

plagues with which the Egyptians were afflicted, the reason being that one's cup of joy cannot be full as long as there is suffering somewhere in the world.

On Purim, when the names of the sons of the archenemy Haman, as they are hanged, are read in the synagogue, the reader must read them all in one breath, for it is painful to consider the torture of even Haman and his sons.

LAWS OF NOACH

In accordance with Jewish law, gentiles are bound by seven general rules of moral conduct. These are called "the seven laws of Noach." They require the setting up of an administration of justice "in all your gates" and forbid murder, incest, robbery, cruelty to animals, idolatry, and blasphemy. They are a comprehensive moral and legal instruction, including hundreds of moral imperatives. These rulings are considered the foundation of human civilization.[20]

Whenever gentiles commit themselves to these seven laws, and decide to settle in the Land of Israel, the Bible states: "He shall dwell with you, in the midst of you in the place which he shall choose, within one of your gates, as it pleases him, you shall not vex him" (Deuteronomy: 23:16-17).

The Rabbis explain:[21] "In the place he shall choose" (where his livelihood is to be found) and "within one of your gates" mean that he is not to be set wandering from place to place. The residents of the town may not complain that he is competing with them in order to force him to move on. On the contrary, they are obligated to sustain him.[22] Thus, the gentile immigrant is entitled to the assistance of the Jewish community to establish himself and his family.

In his Talmud commentary, Rabbi Menahem ben Shlomo

Meiri (thirteenth century) writes,[23] "All who keep the seven commandments are treated equally in the law with us and there is no favoritism for us. It goes without saying that this is so for the nations who are disciplined in the ways of religion and civilization." Why does it go "without saying"? Simply because the great religions demand even more than just the seven commandments. Meiri continues:

> The Almighty will not deprive anyone of reward who engages in Torah for its own sake. It has been expressly said: "Even a non-Jew who engages in Torah, even only in his seven commandments, and even if his nation as a whole transgresses them, since, however, he fulfills them as the Creator's command, he is like the high priest."
>
> Moreover, with regard to the commandments, the Almighty will not deprive of reward those who fulfill them—even for the hurrying to perform a *mitzvah*, though it be not such as needs to be done immediately. It is a great principle for all His commandments: According to a man's work, so shall he be rewarded.

In a monograph that appeared in 1840, Rabbi Zvi Chayes discussed at length Jewish-gentile relations and stated:[24]

> The seven commandments are the natural laws that both Christians and Muhammadans apply in their courts, and both see that they are fulfilled . . . and everyone who keeps the seven commandments, because they were given in God's Torah by the hand of Moses, is a *ger toshav*.[25] Also, Maimonides (Laws of Kings 12) and the Kuzari[26] (4:34) write that these religions are a prelude and a preparation for the anticipated Messiah, who is the principal fruit. Then, they will all become His fruit when they acknowledge Him and the tree will become whole, and they will hold dear the root that they despised at first.

It should, however, be mentioned that the codifiers of the great halachic (Jewish) law state that non-Jews (like Jews) are only to be considered *hasidei umot ha-olam* (righteous gentiles) when they observe these commandments as God-given imperatives and not as "natural law."[27] This means that they must accept the Torah as the word of God of which the seven laws are a part. This includes their acceptance that God gave the Land of Israel as an eternal inheritance to the people of Israel.[28]

CONCLUSION

In conclusion we may state that Israel is a world religion in that it sees the future of mankind as the goal of its pilgrimage. It is a world-transforming nation, often functioning as the guilty conscience of mankind.

It teaches the fatherhood of God and the brotherhood of man. In this sense it is the religion par excellence, since all other religions that made universalism their goal spring from Judaism. It welcomes any righteous gentile to dwell in its country and enjoy full rights.

Its homeland is seen as an eternal inheritance from which it should spread its great message. It guards the garden of the Lord in the name of all nations, to become an eternal spring and fountain from which all men may drink. And many people shall go and say: "Come, let us go up to the mountain of the Lord, to the house of the God of Jacob, and He will teach us of His ways, and we shall walk in His path, for out of Zion shall go forth the Torah and the word of the Lord from Jerusalem" (Isaiah 2:2-3).

6

On the
Israeli-Arab Conflict

A BIBLICAL PERSPECTIVE[1]

An impartial observer of the Middle East will realize that these are unusual times. Tens of thousands of Jews, from many different countries, are returning to their national and historic homeland after thousands of years. Arab states are beginning to reconsider their attitudes toward Israel now that they realize that after more than forty years, Israel is here to stay.

Many gentiles throughout the world show new and keen interest in the Bible, proclaiming fulfillment of the old biblical prophecies. The continuous conflict between the Israelis and the Arabs, specifically the Palestinian Arabs, is constantly the focus of world attention, with more broadcast hours and newspaper column space than any other conflict. It is the most discussed issue at the United Nations and the perceived root of international tension. It is held to have the potential to cause a large-scale Middle East conflict and even a global confrontation. Only in 1994, through intensive negotiations, some kind of a breakthrough *may* have taken place.

The truth is, however, more prosaic. The conflict between the Israelis and the Palestinians is something of a local affair. Looking on the world map, many larger hotbeds can be identified, with even greater issues at stake. For the religious mind all this presents a great challenge. What is the spiritual secret behind this conflict?

From the religious perspective, it seems that another, more profound point is being made. History is not made up of social, political, or economic factors alone, but above all of spiritual forces with far-reaching moral implications. As always, the religious person will turn to the Torah and Jewish tradition, the blueprint of all history and reality, to seek a deeper insight. It is the author's hope that this essay may serve such a purpose.

THE ISRAELI-ARAB CONFLICT

The Torah relates a remarkable sequence of events toward the end of the life of Avraham, the patriarch and founder of world monotheism: "And Avraham had become old and God blessed Avraham with everything" (Genesis: 24:1).

After the death of his beloved wife, Sarah, only one dream remained to be fulfilled: to marry off his son, Yitzchak, in order to fulfill God's promises of spiritual continuity. With that accomplished, Avraham would finally be able to close his eyes and be "gathered to his fathers." And so we read that Avraham sent his faithful servant, Eliezer, to find a wife for Yitzchak. After a long and protracted story, Yitzchak finally marries Rivka.

And the servant related to Yitzchak all the things he had done. And Yitzchak brought her to the tent of his mother,

Sarah, and he married Rivka. She became his wife, and he
loved her, and only then was Yitzchak comforted after his
mother. (Genesis 24:66-67)

Now, finally, Avraham can die peacefully. His life's work
is accomplished. His great mission—to introduce monotheism and justice into this world—has been achieved, and the
future of that mission has been guaranteed through the establishment of the family of Yitzchak. We now anticipate the
moment when the Torah will inform us of the great patriarch's death. However, instead of Avraham dying, we read:
"Then Avraham took a wife again and her name was Keturah.
And she bore him Zimran, Yokshan, Medan, Midyan, Yishbok
and Shuach" (Genesis 25:1-2). Does this not surprise us a
little? We may be justified in asking why Avraham, a tired
old man, should think about getting married again, not to
mention fathering another six children.

If this is not perplexing enough, the Midrash identifies
Avraham's new wife: "Who is Keturah? Hagar!"[2] Hagar, it will
be recalled, had, years earlier, been Avraham's second wife
after Sarah (Genesis 16). But after Hagar had given birth to
Yishmael, Avraham was forced by God to send Hagar and
her son away (Genesis 21). This occurred after protracted
episodes of friction between Sarah and Hagar (Genesis:16)
and after Yishmael threatened to kill Yitzchak.[3]

At this point we are right to be puzzled. Why, after many
years of separation, would Avraham remarry Hagar, the very
woman who had been the cause of so much trouble in the
past? Hagar represents a most tragic and somber moment
in Avraham's life, a tremendous setback accompanied by an
intense feeling of failure. What could be worse for any man,
let alone one epitomizing benevolence and justice, than having to send his wife and child away? It might be further ar-

gued that in remarrying the very woman he had exiled many years earlier, Avraham was only courting disaster and conflict afresh.

In its perplexity, the Midrash asks, Who suggested this *shidduch* (match)? To our surprise we are told that it was Yitzchak's suggestion. Commenting on Genesis 24:62, the *Midrash Rabbah* observes that Yitzchak had been searching for Hagar and brought her to Avraham for a possible marriage.[4] Why would Yitzchak make such a suggestion? What was his motive in raking up the past? After all, it was he who had suffered most bitterly from the whole episode with Hagar.

THE BIRTH OF YITZCHAK

In order to gain an understanding of these complex questions, it is necessary to examine the antecedent history of the relationship between Avraham, Sarah, and Hagar, and of these three protagonists and Yishmael. We read much earlier in the narrative:

> And Sarai, Avram's wife, bore him no children; and she had an Egyptian handmaid whose name was Hagar. And Sarai said to Avram, "See, now, God has restrained me from bearing, I pray thee go in to my maid, perhaps I shall be built through her." And Avram hearkened to the voice of Sarai. (Genesis 16:1-2)

Rabbi Yitzchak Arama, the great fifteenth-century Spanish commentator, when commenting on Genesis 16:2, was perplexed by Sarai's suggestion: "Why did Sarai not ask for children as Rivka did [later on] if she recognized that it was He who denied them to her?"

In other words, did Sarai not have enough trust and belief in God that she could become pregnant and bear a child to Avram? Was it not obvious that all the promises God gave to Avram that he would have a child and be progenitor of a nation meant that Sarai would be the mother?

> And I will make of you a great nation; and I will make your seed as the dust of the earth. (Genesis 15:5)

At the time of this promise, Sarai was Avram's only wife, and it would therefore be very reasonable to maintain that only she would be the mother of Avram's child and future generations. So, why did she ask Avram to marry Hagar?

Rabbi Yitzchak Arama argues that Sarai had very sound reasons for not invoking divine mercy. In referring to the verse (Genesis 18:11), "It had ceased with Sarai to be after the manner with women," he argues that it would have been a mistake for Sarai to beseech God to allow her to become pregnant since this would have involved the violation of the laws of nature. Sarai's postmenopausal physiological condition made it impossible for her to have children unless an open miracle were performed. Based on the principle that *ha-olam be-minhago holech* (the world runs its course in a natural way; i.e., the laws of nature are created as a fixed reality), Sarai reasoned that asking God for pregnancy would be out of order. Miracles occur only when there is no alternative, but in Sarai's mind there was a ready alternative in Hagar. Moreover, Hagar had been raised and educated by Sarai and therefore was, in many ways, her adopted child and pupil. This, reasoned Sarai, was enough to allow Avram to marry Hagar. The child born of this union would, for all intents and purposes, be Sarai's child and would be educated to continue the great mission of Avram.

On a deeper level, it may be suggested that Sarai argued that for the Jewish People to be effective within the world, they had to be born *within* the boundaries of the laws of this world. The child had to be born in a natural way, without any surprising or unprecedented occurrences.

Avram, however, looks beyond. He has been informed that his progeny will have to represent the "beyond." It will have to represent the divine truth, and that truth is not of this world:

> And He [God] took him outside and said, "Look toward the heavens and count the stars if you are able to count them." And He added, "So shall your offspring be." (Genesis 15:5)

On this the Midrash comments: "Did He then lead him forth to the outside of the world. . . . But He showed him the streets of heaven, He lifted him up above the vault of heaven, hence He says to him: "*Habet,*" Look now toward heaven, *Habet,* signifying to look down from above." This midrash clearly implies the metaphysical aspect of the nation to be born. Its root is above the normal and logical.

Only from a heavenly perspective can one understand the essence, the mission, and the most remarkable capacity for survival of the Jewish People. "Look toward heaven" implies the understanding that there is no end to heaven. The innumerable worlds beyond are the root where the foundation of Israel may be discovered. Avram is asked to elevate himself above the finite world.

For this reason Avram cannot agree with Sarai. He waits for the unprecedented, the unusual, and because of all this is convinced that Sarai may still become pregnant. More than that, *because* the nation of Israel must hold the potential to become a metahistorical people, it *had* to be born from the supernatural. It had to be born out of the unprecedented. Therefore, from this perspective, Sarai was the most obvious mother-to-be!

If so, why did Avram not refuse Sarai's request to marry

Hagar? The answer given by Ramban, who posed this question, is that this was only to give Sarai the satisfaction of fulfilling her maternal feelings, but Avram did not believe for one moment that Hagar was ever going to give birth to the child he was promised.[5]

So Avram marries Hagar:

> And Avram hearkened to the voice of Sarai; and Sarai Avram's wife took Hagar, the Egyptian, her maid . . . and gave her to Avram, her husband, to be his wife. (Genesis 16:3)

Then an event happened that caused unexpected complications:

> and when she [Hagar] saw she had conceived, her mistress lost value in her eyes. (Genesis 16:4)

In describing her characteristics, Rabbi Samson Raphael Hirsch notes that the word *hagar* connotes being "bound in," "restrained." Hagar, therefore, is a "limited" woman with little insight into the spiritual and metaphysical world of Avram. She believes that her immediate pregnancy is a sign of personal divine favor and that therefore she, and not Sarai, is the truly righteous woman.

Hagar's philosophy is simple. What she does not understand is that only through trial and hardship does one become a righteous and great personality. An easy life does not produce people of significance. This is the very reason many women in the Torah suffer from the inability to conceive. Only after great effort and spiritual struggles do they give birth to their children.

Hagar, however, is solely of this world and rooted in the natural, and therefore misreads her own story and that of Sarai. We may add that Hagar is a descendant of Cham, the father of Canaan and the second son of Noach. The Torah tells us that after emerging from the ark, Noach planted a vineyard and became "intoxicated" and "uncovered" himself in his tent. Cham saw the "nakedness" of his father and reported the incident to his brothers, Shem and Yaphet (Genesis 9:20-29). One can see in this incident a most important and illuminating fact. Cham, the "heated one," is the one who sees this world from an intoxicated position. He cannot see the deeper meaning of this life; neither does he see that man's bodily appearance is only external and the real man is within. Hagar is, in many ways, a descendant of Cham. She sees the world through Cham's prism and therefore does not grasp Sarai's trial and concomitant greatness. She identifies material success with divine approval, displaying no appreciation for the higher, heavenly world. Due to this perception, she looks down on Sarai.

SARAI'S MISTAKE

Aware of the deep-rooted conflict, Avram gives Sarai carte blanche in her treatment of Hagar:

> And Sarai said to Avram, . . . "I gave my maid unto your bosom and now that she has conceived I have lost value in her eyes." . . . Then Avram said to Sarai: "See your maid is in your hand, do to her that which is good in your eyes." Then Sarai afflicted her and she fled from before her. (Genesis 16:5-6)

Ramban, in his careful reading of the text, makes a most remarkable, indeed, disturbing observation. Instead of trying to justify Sarai's behavior, he condemns her for having mistreated Hagar:

Sarai, our mother, sinned in dealing harshly with her hand-maid and Avram too, by allowing her to do so. [And there-fore] God saw her affliction and gave her a son, who was destined to be a lawless person *who would bring* suffering on the seed of Avram and Sarai with all kinds of *afflictions*.[6] (italics added)

What Ramban is telling us is not just that Sarai had violated the principles of general morality but that she profoundly misunderstood the situation that she herself had created. Rabbi Samson Raphael Hirsch explains:

What she [Sarai] had forgotten is that what she had wished was an impossible thing . . . that a woman—who had become a wife to Avram and a mother to his child could not, on the other hand, be a slave. Avram's proximity and Avram's spirit would break the feelings of slavery, would awaken the feel-ing of the equality of all human beings, would arouse the urge of freedom and break all chains.[7]

Taking this argument one stage further, we may suggest that Sarai had not only misunderstood the personality of Hagar, but above all she failed to realize that the child born from Avram's union with Hagar could only be a highly complex personality.

Many of this child's qualities were rooted in the spiritual world of Avram. But, at the same time, the child would also inherit many of the characteristics of Hagar; in other words, of Cham, the heated one. This inevitably created a most com-plex situation, with incredible tensions and contradictions: a child who would be pained by his inability to identify totally with either Avram's world or Hagar's world—always on the run, never at peace with himself. Sarai did not realize this: Yishmael was going to taste from the wellsprings of Avram's world but would never be completely included in it because of the Chamite mentality. Sarai was playing with fire.

What would have happened if Sarai had allowed herself to properly care for and nurture Yishmael? It is most likely that his personality would have developed differently, having the strength to overcome the inherent tensions within his very being. Rabbi Hirsch postulates that the Arab nation would have become a great asset for the cause of monotheism and religious-ethical life and would have worked hand-in-hand with the People of Israel:

> The nation descended from Avraham and Hagar is one-half Jewish. God has given us, the Jewish nation, a mission, which has a dual aspect: 1. *Emunah*, theoretical truths which we have to accept and which our minds are to develop and 2. *The Law*, the Commandments which in harmonious agreement with these truths form our whole life in accordance with the dictates of the Divine Will. On the one aspect, the theoretical one, the Arabic nation holds a high place in the ranks of mankind. It has developed the Abrahamic thoughts of God with such fine acuteness that the thoughts of the unity of God in the works of Jewish theological philosophers, as far as they are developed philosophically, rest predominantly on the works of Arabian writers. These have the *Emunah* but *not* the *mitzvot*. It is not sufficient to have spiritual thoughts of the unity of God, [but it must include] the practical submission of all forces and efforts [to daily life]. And for that it is not sufficient only to be begotten and brought up by Avraham, for that one must be born from a Sarah. The specific People of Avraham is not given the mission to be the theological philosophical herald of the Unity of God, but *lishmor derech Ha-Shem la'asot tzedakah u'mishpat*, [to guard the way of God and to do righteousness and justice] and that requires the submission of all one's forces, and above all, all one's sensuous forces, urges and impulses, that de-

mands the dedication of the body. One only begins to be Jewish with the dedication of the body.[8]

Had Sarai cared for Yishmael, then the great Arab nation would have had an easier task in fulfilling itself in unprecedented ways, and history would have unfolded in a drastically different way.

Sarai's treatment of Hagar left a permanent rift between the two women, even after Hagar returned home and gave birth to Yishmael (Genesis 16). This sense of hurt and bitterness undoubtedly became imprinted in the mind of the child Yishmael who, thereafter, could only have felt a stranger in the home of Sarai. Somehow, these anti-Sarai feelings were nurtured over the many long years of Yishmael's difficult life, until, as Ramban seems to suggest, they became a permanent mark on the soul of the descendants of Yishmael and developed into an unreasonable hatred for the children of Avraham and Sarai.

Ramban's observation, however, is not without its problems. How does he reconcile his claim here that Sarai was wrong in afflicting Hagar and sending her away, while we read at a later stage (Genesis 21:12) that God concurs with Sarai, telling Avraham to send Hagar and Yishmael away?

After the birth of Yitzchak, tensions intensify between Yishmael and his younger half-brother, reaching such a point that, once again, Sarai asks Avraham to "cast out that slavewoman and her son" (Genesis 21:9). Avraham is greatly distressed, "for it concerned a son of his." Clearly Avraham does not want to have a second tragedy. No father willingly spurns his own son, however wayward. He has learned from the past. Therefore, he refuses to act on Sarai's wish until God indicates His own concurrence: "Whatever Sarai tells you, listen to her voice" (Genesis 21:9).

It appears, then, that Sarai is right after all. Sending Hagar away has God's blessing. If in this instance Sarai is correct, then what was wrong in earlier forcing Hagar out of her house by afflicting her? Did God not further afflict Hagar by making Avraham send her and her son away?

The answer to this question is crystal clear: God tells Avraham that the first expulsion was wrong; it has wrought incredible damage. It has evoked in Hagar and Yishmael an eternal hatred. One cannot turn the clock back. To keep Yishmael home after all that has occurred will only add further complications. Now it is too late. What Avraham has to learn is that there is no way back.

AVRAHAM'S REPENTANCE

We may now begin to arrive at an understanding of our earlier dilemma, namely, why Avraham remarried Hagar at the end of his life. Avraham now realized the enormity of the injustice inflicted on Hagar. The afflictions that she suffered, and subsequently the second expulsion with Yishmael, her son, continued to torment Avraham. In setting his affairs in order before his death, he asks how he—the embodiment of kindness—could have permitted such a thing to occur. How can he meet his Maker without having resolved this problem of his own making? How can he do *teshuvah* (repentance)?

Yitzchak clearly perceives the anguish of his father. He understands that this matter has the potential to become Avraham's downfall. Everything that he had lived for, his devotion to *chesed* (kindness), his piety and all his great acts of righteousness are of little consequence as long as this one matter is not settled. Yitzchak's suggestion that his father remarry his former wife, Hagar, is therefore very understandable. By giving her a few more good years and granting her a happy family life and security, Avraham may be able to make amends, look himself in the face, and meet his Maker with equanimity.

It is therefore not surprising that, on several occasions, Avraham sought out his son Yishmael and advised him whom to marry. However wayward, however unruly, Yishmael was still his son and entitled to Avraham's support.[9]

"PERE ADAM"

While Hagar is in the desert after fleeing (the first time) from Sarai, God appears to her and reveals to her the qualities of the yet unborn child: "He will be like a *pere adam*" (Genesis 16:12). The Rabbis struggle with the exact meaning of these last two words. The classic translation reads "a wild ass," a most disturbing translation.

> Rabbi Yochanan and Resh Lakish debated this. Rabbi Yochanan said: It means that while all people are bred in civilized surroundings, he would be reared in the wilderness. Resh Lakish said: It means a savage among men, in its literal sense, for as all people plunder wealth, he plunders lives. (*Genesis Rabbah* 35:9)

Rabbi Hirsch adds, "He will not be just *adam pere* a free man, he will be *pere adam*, the *pere* amongst mankind . . . such a race of men who do not bow their necks to the yoke of other men."[10]

God continues,

> His hand against every man, and every man's hand against him, and in the face of all his brothers will he dwell. (Genesis 16:12)

This could mean that he will stand up against his own brothers and cause instability in the Arab world. It may also refer to his constant struggles with the nations of the world.

Da'at Sofrim on Genesis 16:12 explains the prophecy further: "Although he will be a man with great potential, intellect and emotions, his hand will be against everybody, and everybody against him, and still: 'In the face of all his brothers will he dwell,' i.e:, he will be honored by all the nations." Ramban expands the argument: "The subject pertains to his children, who will increase and they will have wars with all the nations."

Such prophecies and interpretations do not imply that Yishmael *has* to become as described in these prophecies; neither do the earlier observations justify the Arab animosity toward Jews in our days or at any other time. The injustice of Sarah toward Yishmael cannot be used as a precedent for an ongoing hatred toward the children of Avraham and Sarah.

These observations and visions draw attention to the roots from where these feelings come. They indicate that these prophecies *will* become true if Yishmael will yield to these dispositions instead of fighting them. Man's chief goal in life is to become human and to protect his humanity against these kinds of tendencies. Would Yishmael understand this and fight these inclinations, or redirect them, he could no doubt become a most eloquent and highly civilized man.

The above-quoted prophetic descriptions are made from a combination of dispositions that make up the personality of Yishmael. On the one hand, they are rooted in the world of Avraham, while on the other, they stem from the world of Cham.

Perseverance, courage, and independence are the very

qualities that Avraham developed in order to fulfill his mission to bring all men to a recognition of God. Once, however, these qualities become misdirected and absorbed by the world of Cham, they start to serve external and physical purposes such as military power and willful stubbornness. The very propensity for domination found within the Arab world, harnessed to the vast financial resources at its disposal, is the result of the qualities inherent in Avraham's spiritual mission becoming misdirected. When these qualities are used for purely earthly causes, as is the case with the Chamite philosophy, they become dangerous and destructive. The Arab will to dominate, with its bold and daring (and often self-destructive) courage, when combined with autonomous philosophies, are therefore basically misdirected qualities inherited from Avraham.

WORLD DOMINATION

At this point it would be pertinent to investigate another feature of our global question. From the above verses it can be clearly deduced that the descendants of Yishmael would like to dominate the world and create an independent world power. We may ask how one ever becomes a *world-dominating* power. In other words, how does one "possess" the world? What are the ways in which to seize the very powers by which this world is set into motion?

Jewish tradition believes that this is accomplished by possessing the Land of Israel, and specifically, Jerusalem. Jerusalem we are told, is built on the *even shetiah*, the foundation stone. The Talmud, in *Yoma* 54b, states that it was so called because "from it the world was founded." Rashi, in his commentary to this statement, adds, "Zion was first created, and then around it other clods and rock formations; continents were formed until the earth was complete."

Ramban, commenting on the first verse of the Torah and reflecting kabbalistic teachings, writes, "Jerusalem is the pre-eminent place, for the life of the world starts there, its potential is developed therein, its climates and the species of all orders appear in it."

Jerusalem is seen, therefore, as the root of all places. The Land of Israel, the first extension of Jerusalem, is the soul of the world. It is the *Holy Land*—set apart and sanctified from the rest of the world. It is the world in microcosm in which all the components of the greater world are represented. It is the *kav emtza'i*, the medium line, "the inner, spiritual bolt that contains everything that connects all points of the world among themselves to the original point."[11]

This is the reason the nations of the world have always maintained their focus on Jerusalem and Israel. Subconsciously, they have been aware that, somehow, possession of this city and this land meant "controlling" the world. The essence of the world is virtually contained in Jerusalem. Obviously, this means that Jerusalem and Israel are the center of this world in the spiritual sense. It is from there that the teachings of the Torah will come and transform the world. However, the many nations that once occupied the Land of Israel translated this "inner knowledge" into terms of purely physical occupations, without understanding the spiritual implications.

In the case of the Arab nations, this matter is even more apparent. As children of Avraham, the status and "ownership" of the Land of Israel becomes a matter of crucial importance. Their longing for this land is not just bound up with their ambition to become a world power like other nations of the world. It is the consequence of Avraham's mission to trans-

form that makes the impetus to possess this land so powerful. As explained above, it is this mission, albeit misdirected
by Chamite influence, that makes the Arab world seek ways
to "inherit" the land and overpower the world. It is this matter
that makes the Israeli-Arab conflict so complex.

What are the conditions by which one can permanently
hold on to, and secure, the Land of Israel, and thereby really
"inherit" it? Such a matter is not decided on the basis of history or political force alone.

According to biblical thought, it will depend greatly on
the spiritual and moral condition of the "occupier." The land
itself, being the "center" of the world, is like Jerusalem, also
called *Sha'ar Ha-Shamaim* (the gateway to heaven). Jerusalem is a heavenly city. It is the city where the Sanctuary is
found with the Holy of Holies, in which there is no time and
no space limitation. It is often referred to as Heavenly Jerusalem; it is *le-ma'ala min ha-tevah* (beyond nature). It is heaven
reflected in earthly conditions. Consequently, only a nation
that is rooted in, and living by, the "norms" of heaven will
be capable of possessing this land and this city.

Discussing the *mitzvah* (commandment) of *olei regel*, or
going up to Jerusalem to celebrate the festivals in the Temple,
the Torah states, "No man will covet your land when you
ascend to appear before the Lord three times a year" (Exodus 34:24).

The implication of this unusual verse is that while all
Jews go to the Temple on Pesach, Shavuot, and Sukkot, the
borders of the Land of Israel may be in grave danger. It would
be an open invitation for the enemies of Israel to cross the
borders and force the People Israel out of their homeland.
Nevertheless, the Torah avers that not only will the enemies
not enter the land but they would not even consider making such a move. This is a most extraordinary and unnatural

promise and against our general experience. Why should they not consider such an option? Why would they not even consider coveting the land?

According to our observations, we may understand what the Torah is driving at. When the Jews ascend to "appear before the Lord," namely, when their lives are built on the principles that the Temple represents, *only then* will it be clear and undisputed who holds the title to this land. When Israel views its national life from "beyond" and is fully aware of, and lives up to, its great mission, it will experience peace on all its borders. This land can only be owned by those whose lives are in accordance with its spiritual nature. Otherwise other nations will claim it. The moment, however, that the spiritual standards of the Land of Israel are met, these nations will no longer aspire to possess it.

This, then, is the great prophecy behind the above verse: *Only the people of Israel, adhering to the Torah of Israel, hold title to the Land of Israel.* This may quite well be the "biblical" message behind the Israeli-Arab conflict.

7

On the Primordial Torah

ne of the most distinctive features of traditional Judaism is the awe with which it regards the Written Torah (Pentateuch). This reverence flows from an uncompromising insistence that the text of the Torah is not the product of some human mind but is rather a creation of God. According to this belief, God explicitly dictated to Moshe not only every one of the letters and words of the Torah but even the crowns that are placed above some of its letters.[1]

The knowledge found in the Torah is therefore believed to be of supreme value. A man or woman can, through the careful study of its narratives and the meticulous observance of its *mitzvot* (commandments), be lifted beyond the mundane world until he or she is able to grasp the ineffable and the eternal. One will furthermore be inspired to live a life of sanctification and moral greatness, rising to ever higher levels of righteousness.

There is, however, another, hidden aspect of the Torah, which has been revealed only by the masters of the Kabbalah, the mystical tradition of Judaism. They teach us that the Torah contains meanings far beyond its usually revealed ethical and spiritual ones. They tell us that the Torah is the repository of an all-encompassing knowledge embracing not only religious tradition but also such matters as science, philosophy, psychology, and history. It furthermore includes information that the human intellect could not discover by itself: information about all that has transpired or will transpire during the existence of the entire universe, and even secrets of the mystical worlds that precede and transcend ours.

This assertion of the all-inclusiveness of the Torah is not a new one. The kabbalists find it already mentioned in the Mishnah, one of the earliest authoritative Jewish sources, which is accepted as being the authentic formulation of an unbroken tradition extending back to the giving of the Torah at Sinai. In *Pirke Avot*, Ben Bag-Bag, a scholar and teacher who lived in the Land of Israel in the first century C.E., says of the Torah, "*Delve into it again. Use it to see the truth, for all is in it. Grow old in it, and depart not from it, there is no better pursuit for you than the Torah.*"[2] (italics added)

This assertion that *all* is in the Torah strikes the uninitiated, if he is kindly predisposed, as an exaggeration, and if he is not, as manifest proof of the philosophically untenable basis of Jewish thought. The world is so vast and complex that even the sum total of all that men have labored to write throughout thousands of years is inadequate to describe it. Therefore, the rational mind finds it simply impossible to believe that this one small book, the Torah, can contain everything. Nevertheless the Kabbalah insists that the Torah indeed does contain all that can be known about this universe—and about any other.

For the kabbalists, the fact that the casual reader will find none of this knowledge in the Torah is not seen as a refutation of this concept. On the contrary, it is understood that most of this vast knowledge is not to be found there on an explicit level. Rather, in the Written Torah, God has created a structure of infinite depth and complexity, in which it will always be possible to discover new levels of meaning. Thus, the scholars and Sages of every generation will be able to labor all their lives to understand it yet still leave unsuspected aspects to be revealed by generations to come. In short, according to this point of view, the reason man does not see all the infinite knowledge contained in the Torah is simply that man, being finite, does not have infinite perception.

All these ideas call for more explanation. Fortunately, such explication is plentifully available in the Kabbalah and the Midrash. To understand these traditions, we must first examine how Judaism deals with the phenomenon of divine speech, with the fact that the infinite Creator was able to communicate with mere flesh and blood.

MONOLOGUE AND DIALOGUE

Human beings make use of two modes of "speech," which may be called creative monologue and dialogue. A person may engage in creative monologue without formulating his thoughts into words. He is not concerned to be understood or appreciated. He "speaks" because of the overflow of a creative impetus within himself.

When a person engages in dialogue, either with another individual or with an audience (as when a teacher addresses his students), the essential aim is communication. Concern with the audience's level of comprehension is therefore of utmost importance. The listener's interest, intellectual capacity, and language limitations significantly influence the

method that must be used to transmit the message successfully. The speaker must simplify the content and often drastically reorganize the format of his discourse.

These two modes, creative monologue and dialogue, are
successive steps in a process of externalization. The monologue may exist by itself, but the dialogue cannot take place
unless preceded by the monologue, for the ideas that the
speaker expresses in his language of dialogue must first have
taken form in the private creative monologue of his mind.
On the basis of this distinction, we may come to understand
the difference between the "speech" with which God called
the world into existence and that with which He conveyed
His will to the Israelite nation at Sinai.

At the time of the Creation, God spoke in the monologue mode. He brought the universe into existence through
a unique form of creative activity that, because of its transcendent nature, could not be understood by any outsider.
At that time He expressed Himself in a divine monologue
incomprehensible to the human intellect. At Sinai, however,
God spoke in the dialogue mode. His audience waited for
His words of guidance. In order for them to comprehend His
message, He had to adapt His speech to their intellect. Thus,
He spoke in a language of communication. Only here, in the
Pentateuch, was the act of creation translated into human
words: "Let there be. . . . "

THE PRIMORDIAL TORAH

The dichotomy between the two divine languages of monologue and dialogue is the underlying principle behind one
of the most remarkable concepts in kabbalistic thought: the
claim that there exists not one Torah, but two.

The first Torah is called the *Torah Kedumah*, the Primordial Torah. The second is the Written Torah, which was received at Sinai. It is called the Torah of Moses, the Pentateuch. This may be termed the Human Torah. A closer examination of the relationship between these two *Torot* reveals that the Human Torah emerges from the Primordial Torah in much the same way that the language of dialogue emerges from that of monologue.

The Primordial Torah is an infinite expression of the transcendent being of God. It reflects God in His essence, the secret world of His wisdom, untouched by the dimensions of human understanding. The Primordial Torah is the product of God in direct conversation with Himself, expressing the mysterious totality of His being. Not surprisingly, then, some kabbalistic schools have suggested that the Primordial Torah in some enigmatic way can be thought of as God's "mind." Of this *Torah Kedumah* it is said: "*The Torah is not something outside God, and He is not outside the Torah.*"[3] (italics added) The Sages refer to this infinite aspect of Torah when they say: "*God looked into the Torah and created the world.*"[4] (italics added)

It goes without saying that the document written with ink on parchment is not to be thought of literally as being an embodiment of God's mind. Neither is it possible to imagine that God in all His glory needs a book to instruct Him. Therefore, it is obvious that the Torah referred to is an eternally preexisting entity: the Primordial Torah. In a remarkable midrash, the Sages deal with the relationship between the Primordial Torah and the Human Torah, as these manifested themselves at Sinai. "*The Torah that God gave to Moshe was given to him as white fire engraved by black fire. It is fire mixed with fire, cut from fire, and given from fire.*"[5] (italics added)

The Sages of the Midrash, when expressing the most profound matters, communicate with extraordinary brevity, preferring to use a unique kind of allegory rather than presenting abstract concepts as Western philosophy does. Thus, in the Midrash, the Torah is characterized symbolically as fire. The white fire corresponds to the Primordial Torah and the black fire to the Human Torah.

As a first step in the revelation at Sinai, as described by this midrash, Moshe was granted a vision that no other human being either before or since has seen: a glimpse of the pure, white fire of the Primordial Torah. He was granted this vision in order to impress upon him the magnitude of the gift that he was about to receive.

This does not mean that Moshe saw the *Torah Kedumah* itself, since this is nothing less than God's transcendent mind, which is hidden from all His creation. Rather, he saw its reflection or shadow, as expressed in the white fire. This was enough to impress upon him the awesomeness and immensity of the actual, hidden Primordial Torah.

However, this was only the beginning of the revelation. For the Torah in this inchoate form was far from being the Torah that God intended the Children of Israel to receive. Although Moshe was able to perceive something of it, the *Torah Kedumah* conveyed no relevant message to him. It was still in a form that was only comprehensible to the divine mind.

Therefore, a process began that would bring the Torah closer to human understanding. In the language of the Midrash, the white fire ("It is fire . . . ") was made to differentiate itself into elements ("mixed with fire . . ."). Instead of being a pure, transcendent unity, it began to have recognizable parts—the two fires. The differentiation was the second stage of the adaptation of the divine mind to the human level.

The allegory is clear. Torah, the divine mind, is symbolized as fire, the most intangible of elements. Like fire, it cannot be contained or divided. The miracle of the giving of Torah is that this fire has been given a new form. It has become "fire mixed with fire," black fire mixed with white fire.

At first the black fire and the white fire were a simple duality, black on white, but as the vision continued, the black fire began slowly to form itself into a configuration of Hebrew letters. This development is described in further detail by other kabbalistic sources, as follows: The first letters to take form were those of the Tetragrammaton. This is the ultimate metaphysical Name, the essential appellation of the transcendent Creator. From these four letters emerged the remaining letters of the Hebrew alphabet. *Sefer Yetzirah* tells us that the letters danced, joining into hundreds of combinations, starting with those of two letters—אא, בא, אב—and evolving progressively into longer combinations. These permutations became the names of God through which all the phenomena of the universe were created. These names are primal elements of creation.[6] They no longer represent God's essential Name but rather the basic forces through which He creates the multiplicity of the universe. They are the DNA code, the code from which everything emerges. Just as a DNA molecule is made from a very small number of basic elements, yet contains in capsule form all the knowledge that is needed to produce a living being, so these permutations of spiritual energies, which Moshe perceived as Hebrew letters, contained the whole universe: "*The letters of the [Primordial] Torah are the basis of every creation and the source of every phenomenon. Just as they form endless unique permutations, so each worldly phenomenon is composed of a unique combination of elements . . . in such a way that no two beings are identical.*"[7] (italics added)

Some of these permutations were recognizable names of God, such as *Elohim*, *El*, and *Shaddai*. Others were combinations of letters without meaning in human language. But all of them were divine names, conduits through which the divine creative power flows to the creation. This was another step in the process of humanization of the Torah. There were words, but no language; spiritual energies, but no fixed pattern.

As the letters of the black fire continued to permute into longer and longer configurations, they began to form themselves into one tremendous word, one long Name containing all the permutations of letters that had appeared previously. The Kabbalah states that this Name of God was made from none other than the order of letters comprising the text of the Torah as we know it today. It is to this aspect of the Torah that the *Zohar* refers when it states, "*The entire Torah is a single, holy, mystical Name.*"[8] (italics added)

Among the classical medieval commentators on the Torah, it was Nachmanides (Ramban) who elaborated on this final form that the black fire took in Moshe's vision. He speaks of it in the introduction to his commentary on the Torah:

> It would appear that in the Torah written with letters of black fire upon a background of white fire the writing was contiguous, without being broken up into words. This made it possible to be read either according to the division into divine names or according to our normal reading, which makes explicit the Torah and the commandments. Both interpretations were given to our teacher Moshe: the division of words that express the commandments was given to him in written form, and the rendition that consists of the divine names was transmitted to him orally.[9]

Ramban tells us that Moshe was given two ways of interpreting this final great Name of God. The first was the division into words of our Written Torah, in Ramban's language the "commandments," the law for man. The second was a secret key by which this same text could be used to reveal the mysteries of the divine names.

This key consisted of various esoteric methods of rearranging and interpreting the letters of the great Name. Among these techniques are recombining letters (*tzeruf*), interpreting the numerical values of letters and words (*gematria*), and constructing acrostics using the initial or final letters of words.

In a similar vein *Sefer Sha'arei Orah* says:

> The whole [written] Torah is a fabric of divine attributes (*kinnuyim*, [secondary names]). These in turn are woven from the various [primal] names of God [the permutations of the Hebrew alphabet of the Primordial Torah], which in turn are connected to and resolve back into the Tetragrammaton [י-ה-ו-ה].
>
> Thus the entire Torah is ultimately woven from the Tetragrammaton.[10]

Although the Torah had finally coalesced into a form amenable to human consciousness, it remained simultaneously a reflection of the divine mind. Just as the divine mind contains the ultimate knowledge, encompassing all other knowledge, so the person who has the key to the divine names of the Primordial Torah has access to all the knowledge of the universe.

Once we have understood this, it should no longer be surprising to us that the Sages of the Kabbalah, who have received this key by word of mouth through the generations, state that everything knowable by the human mind can be found in the Torah.

THE TORAH OF MOSHE

The insights gained thus far allow us to understand the biblical narratives and commandments on a more profound level. Many consider the Torah valuable chiefly for its historical and moral implications. The Torah definitely includes these aspects. It is understood by Jewish tradition to be an accurate historical record, and its moral teachings are certainly of supreme value. However, the Torah contains much more.

As described earlier, the biblical narratives and commandments are representations of God's thoughts in human language. And even more—every sentence and word, every nuance and repetition, represent a metaphysical world. The meaning of the episodes thus goes far beyond their historical and moral value. Adam and Eve confronting the snake in the garden, Noach in his ark, or Avraham asking Sarai to prepare a meal for his guests reflect a hidden spiritual reality. When people study these narratives, they are treading pathways that make the world of higher truth accessible. These stories and their personages break through the mundane meaning of their historical reality and soar into the stratosphere of esoteric knowledge.

Avraham, for example, is not just a private person living his life but also a paradigmatic figure who adumbrates in his actions the fate of the Jewish People until the end of time. On a still deeper level he is the embodiment, in human form, of one of the divine attributes: that of loving-kindness (*chesed*). Finally, the very words and letters of his story are permutations of names of God, comprising infinitely deep metaphysical knowledge. Jewish tradition speaks of this multileveled structure of meanings as the Pardes (Orchard). The fruit in this orchard provides a glimpse into the divine mind.

These deep metaphysical secrets can be derived only through the text of the Written Torah that was given at Sinai, the text that compromises the great Name reflecting the mind of God. It is therefore not surprising that Jewish tradition has placed such an emphasis on preserving the Written Torah with uncompromising accuracy. Nachmanides (Ramban) writes, in the same introduction to the Torah that was quoted previously:

> [We are obliged, for example,] to disqualify a scroll of the law in which the letter *vav* (ו) is missing from the word *otam* in one of the thirty-nine places where this word is fully spelled out. Similarly disqualified is a scroll in which a *vav* was added to this word in one of the many places where it should be written without *vav*.[11]
>
> This is the rule in all such cases, even though the change in spelling does not change the meaning. It is for this reason that the great Sages who dealt with the scriptural text, of whom the first was the prophet Ezra the Scribe, counted every place where a word is spelled "full" or "short" in the Torah, as well as in the other scriptural texts, and wrote books about these calculations.[12]

In fact, Jewish tradition insists not only that every letter but even that every detail, down to the "crowns" attached to certain letters (as mentioned above), must remain sacrosanct, since all are supercharged with meaning.

When questioning the truthfulness of the Torah or the historical accuracy of its narratives, people ask whether the Garden of Eden really existed and whether Avraham was a real person. They ask whether there was really a flood in the days of Noach and how the Children of Israel were able to cross the Red Sea without getting wet.

We believe these are not the real questions. Even

though Jewish tradition asserts the historicity of the biblical narratives, the crucial question is whether these convey
truth that transcends the historical dimension: do they reflect truth as found in the mind of the Creator? Once this
has been affirmed, the historicity of the biblical narratives
follows as a necessary corollary, for history itself, like the
Torah, is nothing more than a manifestation of God's mind.
We may now return to Ben Bag Bag's credo: "*Delve into it
again and again. Use it to see the truth; for all is in it. Grow
old in it, and depart not from it, for there is no better pursuit
for you than Torah.*"

We can now see why such importance has been placed
through the ages on studying the Torah. Since it is a manifestation of the divine mind on the human level, its study
assumes a dimension totally different from disciplines produced by the human mind. The person who devotes himself to penetrating the depths of the Torah internalizes the
supreme knowledge. Through it one is able to be purified
by attaching oneself to the Eternal.

We can also understand why the Jewish tradition holds
the proponents of literary criticism of the Bible in such con-
tempt. Bible criticism claims to invalidate the divine authorship of the Pentateuchal text by pointing out its seeming contradictions, repetitions, and differences in style. On this basis
it is claimed that the Torah is a composite text, containing
sections written by a number of authors, and even worse,
that it is abundant with scribal errors and revisions added at
a far later date. These arguments lose all credibility once we
understand the true nature of the Torah. Its textual structure, with its sometimes abbreviated, sometimes elaborate
language, is a necessary vehicle for the expression of the divine mind in all its dimensions. Thus, this text cannot be approached using the same criteria one would apply to other

texts. It is as if one were to apply the laws governing inorganic matter when trying to understand the inner workings of a highly developed living being.[13]

MOSHE AND THE ANGELS

All this may throw some light on another tradition found in the Talmud. R. Yehoshua ben Levi said:

When Moshe ascended to the heavenly realms, the angels who served there in the Divine Presence [protested] saying:
"Lord of the Universe, what is a human being doing among us?"
"He has come to receive the Torah," answered God.
They responded: "How can You be giving to creatures of flesh and blood this beloved treasure, which You kept to Yourself for nine hundred and seventy-four generations before the creation of the world?"
God said to Moshe: "You answer them."
Moshe replied: "I am afraid that they will burn me with the fire of their mouths."
He told him: "Hold on to My throne of glory and give them an answer."
Moshe said to God: "Lord of the Universe, what is written in the Torah that You are giving me? 'I am the Lord your God, who took you out of the land of Egypt.'" He then turned to the angels.
"Did you go down to Egypt? Were you Pharaoh's slaves? What good is the Torah to you? What else is written there? 'You shall have no other gods besides Me!' Do you live among the gentiles who serve idols [that you must be warned against them]? What else is written there? 'Remember the Sabbath day to sanctify it!' Do you ever work that you should need a day of rest? . . ."

On hearing these words the angels immediately admitted to the Holy one, Blessed be He, that He was right to give the Torah to Moshe.[14]

We may wonder what the Sages who related this story had in mind when they envisioned Moshe disputing with the angels. How could the angels even have suggested that the Torah should remain exclusive property of the heavenly realms? Was it not clear that the contents of this text could refer only to mankind?

Our earlier observations may very well contain the explanation. The Angels thought that God was about to give Moshe the Torah that they knew, possibly the Torah of divine names. The text of this Torah consists of the same letters as the Human Torah, but it expresses far more deep concepts. This version of the Torah is appropriate only to those who serve before the exalted divine throne. Mankind would find it incomprehensible. And even if man could understand it, access to the metaphysical powers expressed in the divine names should not be given to a creature whose concern is also the care of his physical body. It would be dangerous for the existence of the world if the powers of creation and destruction were given into the hands of a creature who finds it difficult to distinguish between good and evil.

Moshe was actually shown this Torah of the divine names and may have partially grasped its secrets. The human mind, however, does not normally have the power to apprehend it. Therefore, in the Written Torah the letters were regrouped into human words, relating humanly relevant narratives such as that of the Exodus from Egypt and laws applicable to the human condition such as the observance of the day of rest. It was only after Moshe informed the angels of this version that they realized their reading remained untouched by man, and as such could remain in its angelic heaven.

THE TORAH OF THE MESSIANIC AGE

We will now examine an example of the classical kabbalistic literature. It incorporates one of the techniques, taught to Moshe, by which the letters of our Torah are rearranged in order to reveal its metaphysical aspects. This example is found in the famous work *Chesed Le-Avraham*, by Rabbi Avraham Azulai. There it is attributed to his teacher, one of the last and most prolific of the early kabbalists, Rabbi Moshe Cordovero. The technique used is *tzeruf* or recombining of letters. This method is employed to resolve the seeming contradiction of two fundamental Jewish concepts.

The first of these concepts is that the Torah and its *mitzvot* (commandments) are eternal. This principle is clearly expressed by Maimonides (Rambam) in his masterwork, the *Mishneh Torah*:

> It is clearly and explicitly stated in the Torah that its law will endure forever and ever and will undergo no change, diminution, or augmentation, as it is said: "Whatever I command you, you shall be careful to do; you shall not add to it or detract from it" (Deuteronomy 13:1).[15]

This is understood by Jewish tradition to mean that the Jewish People are committed to observe all the commandments at all times, in all places, and under all conditions. Hence, the commandments are applicable not only today but in the Messianic Age as well. However, it is also told in Jewish tradition that when the world reaches its final era of perfection, man will no longer be dominated by his evil inclination (*yetzer ha-ra*).[16] At the same time, the *yetzer ha-ra* will exist in a much more sublimated form. It makes little sense to prohibit murder and sexual license in a world where the desire to commit these acts no longer exists in the human personality.

This is our contradiction: on the one hand, it is claimed that the *mitzvot* will endure forever, and on the other hand, that many will lose their meaning for the highly spiritual messianic man. This very same contradiction also arises in relationship to the earliest periods of man's existence, at which time he was also free of the evil inclination as we know it today. We read at the beginning of the Torah, "*And God took Adam and placed him in the Garden of Eden to work and guard it*" (Genesis 2:15).

The Sages ponder about the way in which Adam and Eve "worked" and "guarded" this garden. Why was it necessary to work and guard the garden? Was not everything there ready for man, making physical labor unnecessary? Since it is therefore impossible to say that the work referred to in the verse was physical labor in the garden, the Sages concluded that it was in the Torah that they "worked" and its commandments that they "guarded."[17]

This interpretation no doubt offers a general solution to the questions of the Sages. But it raises a still more difficult question, very similar to the one we have raised in connection with the messianic man: What Torah did Adam and Eve study, and which commandments did they keep? As long as they had not tasted of the forbidden fruit, they were living in a state similar to the one in which we will live in the Messianic Age. They were higher souls, as yet undamaged by the lower urges that the post-Garden of Eden man encounters. As such they were not in need of the commandments found in the Torah.

Since these two questions regarding the nature of the Torah before the Fall and its character in the Messianic Age are essentially one, we should not be surprised to find that the Kabbalah offered essentially the same solution to both.

The Kabbalah teaches that the original couple living in

the garden had a higher version of the Torah. This version was relevant to their exalted level, a level situated between man and angels. It was this Torah that they worked with and guarded—and it is this Torah as well that man will encounter in the Messianic Age:

> In regard to the new interpretations of the Torah that God will reveal in the Messianic Age, we may say that the Torah remains eternally the same but that in the beginning [after the Fall] it assumed the form of material combinations of letters that were adapted to the material world. However, some day men will cast off this material body. At that time they will be transfigured and recover the mystical body that was Adam's before the Fall. They will understand the mysteries of the Torah and its hidden aspects will be made manifest. Later, at the end of the sixth millennium [after the true messianic redemption], when man becomes a still higher spiritual being, he will penetrate still deeper into the hidden mystery of the Torah.
>
> Then everyone will be able to understand the miraculous content of the Torah and the secret combination of letters of which it is composed and will thereby learn much concerning the secret essence of the universe. . . . For the Torah, like man himself, put on a material garment in order to come into this world. In the same way, when man rises up from his material garments (that is, his corporeal condition) to a more spiritual one, the material manifestation of the Torah will also be transformed. Then its spiritual essence will be apprehended in ever rising degrees. . . . The veiled faces of the Torah will become radiant and the righteous will study them. Yet in all these stages the Torah will be the same as it was in the beginning; its essence will never change.[18]

We now understand in what way the Torah as a whole is said to be eternally relevant, since it will be perceived differently by man when he rises to a higher spiritual level. But

what, one may ask, will become of the individual commandments after this metamorphosis? Will they altogether disappear? In that case there remains unresolved the earlier-
mentioned contradiction concerning the eternal applicability
of the commandments.

We now come to the solution offered by Rabbi Moshe
Cordovero. He provides us with an extremely interesting
example of how a specific commandment would have been
applicable even in the Garden of Eden. From this we can see
how the same commandment would apply in the Messianic
Age. He discusses the biblical prohibition of *sha'atnez*, the
wearing of clothes made of wool mixed with linen:

> The Torah (Deuteronomy 22:11) says: "Thou shall not wear
> *sha'atnez*." This could not have been written before Adam
> himself had clad himself in the coarse material stuff of which
> this world is made, which in mystical language is known as
> "the skin of the serpent." Thus, his Torah could not have
> contained such a prohibition, for what bearing could this
> *sha'atnez* have had on the soul of man, who was originally
> clothed in a purely spiritual garment?
>
> The fact is that the original combination of letters in the
> verse describing the *mitzvah* of *sha'atnez* in the Torah be-
> fore the Fall was not the one we find in our Torah, that is,
> שעטנז צמר ופשתים (*sha'atnez tzemer u-fishtim* ["mixture of wool
> and linen"]). Although the verse there contained the same
> consonants as it does in our version, they were put in an-
> other combination, שטן עז מצר ותפשים (*Satan az metzar u-tofsim*
> ["insolent Satan afflicts and they ensnare"]).
>
> In this form the commandment was a warning to Adam
> not to exchange his original garment of light for the garment
> of serpent's skin, representing the evil power named *Satan
> az* (insolent Satan). Further, the words embody a warning
> to the effect that these powers would assuredly bring fear

and affliction, מצר (metzar) upon man and that they would attempt to ensnare him (ותפשים, u-tofsim), and thereby bring him
down to Gehenna.

What brought about the change in the combination of
letters so that we now read, שעטנז צמר ופשתים (sha'atnez tzemer
u-fishtim)? When Adam put on the "skin of the serpent" his
nature became material, necessitating a Torah that gave
material commandments. This called for a new reading of
the letters to convey the meaning of the commandments.
Similarly, all the other commandments adapted themselves
to the corporeal and material nature of man.[19]

The observant reader will note that both the form taken
by the mitzvah of sha'atnez in this world and the form taken
in the worlds of perfection express one and the same basic
idea: that God has defined distinct domains within His creation, each with its own characteristics and functions, and
that these domains must not be confused with each other.
In our Torah these domains are symbolized by the plant
world, represented by linen, and the animal world, represented by wool. In the higher version of the Torah the two
worlds are the material, in which we wear, metaphorically
speaking, the garment of the serpent, and the spiritual, in
which we wear garments of pure light. Thus messianic man,
like Adam, will still be required to observe the prohibition
of sha'atnez, but on a far more spiritual level.

We see from this that the Torah of the Messianic Age
will be essentially identical to ours. The letters will be the
same, they will simply be divided into words in a different
manner, with minor changes in the order of the letters. However, the mitzvot will remain, though lifted up to a spiritual
level relevant to the new era.

All of this is very well summarized by the most famous
of all kabbalists, Rabbi Isaac Luria, the Arizal:

Just as Adam's body before the sin was much more exalted
than it was afterward, the Torah he was given in the Garden
of Eden to "work and guard" had a higher form than the one
it took later. In just the same way, all the effort a person puts
into observing the commandments in this world is in order
to create for himself a splendid spiritual garment, and in order
that he should merit to enter into the earthly paradise dressed
in it. There, he will "work and guard" the Torah just as the
Blessed One intended . . . when He created Adam.[20]

Torah in the Messianic Age is, in fact, a reflection of an
even higher version, which finds its roots in the Primordial
Torah, the mind of God. Thus, all the commandments will be
transformed when the world reaches a higher spiritual level.
Such a transformation, however, will only take place once the
Messianic Age becomes a reality. In the meantime, the commandments, as performed today, retain their absolute validity.

The rabbinical principle that it is forbidden to write vo-
calization or punctuation marks in a Torah scroll suddenly
becomes more meaningful. Its purpose is to prevent the biblical text from becoming "frozen" to such an extent that other,
higher, readings become impossible. As long as the Torah is
in a form without punctuation, it remains flexible enough to
reveal other aspects of the Primordial Torah, such as the Torah
of the Garden of Eden and the Torah of the Messianic Age.

THE ORAL TORAH

Until this point the discussion has been confined to the Written Torah. However, there is yet another level in the humanization of the mind of God. This is the Oral Torah. Jewish
tradition maintains that the Oral Torah was given together
with the Written Torah at Sinai. After all, the Written Torah,

even though it has already taken the form of human stories and commandments, is still incomprehensible without the oral commentary. Thus it has been an essential task of the Sages to preserve the Oral Torah. This they have done in a vast literature, stretching from the Talmud to the codes of Jewish law, and onward to today's halachic authorities.

The Written Torah is essentially fixed and unchangeable. By Jewish law, not a single letter can be altered. The Oral Torah, on the other hand, is just what its name implies: a tradition passed on by word of mouth from master to disciple. Hence, it is always flexible and adaptable. While the basic content does not change, each teacher can choose whatever words and style he prefers. Until one knows something of this Oral Torah and how it relates to the Written Torah, one will remain lacking in understanding of the Jewish attitude toward the Torah as a whole.

To understand the significance of the Oral Torah, one must return to the symbol of the white and the black fires. Until now these two fires have been identified as representing the Primordial Torah and the Human Torah. Surprisingly, however, the kabbalistic masters sometimes maintain that these same fires also represent the Written Torah and the Oral Torah, respectively:

> In God's right hand were engraved the forms of all the vehicles for communicating His wisdom that were destined some day to emerge from potential to actual. . . . The two principle forms that were engraved there were the Written Torah and the Oral Torah. The Written Torah was engraved there in white fire and the Oral Torah was engraved there in black fire.[21]

This new use of the symbol of the white and black fires raises a paradox. The white fire previously represented the

Primordial Torah, which cannot be captured in writing. Now it is said to represent the Written Torah, whose essence is writing! The black fire previously represented the Written Torah. Now it is said to represent the Oral Torah, which is essentially unwritten! Upon closer examination, however, readers will find that this new interpretation of the two fires is not a paradox at all but rather an extension of principles that were discussed earlier.

When the kabbalistic passage speaks of the "Written Torah," it does not mean the Human Torah, which is written with ink on parchment. Rather, it refers to the Primordial Torah, the expression of God's mind. Why, then, is it called "written"? Because, just as the Written Torah is fixed and unalterable, so is the Primordial Torah. It represents the final, unalterable outcome of God's creative process.

Similarly, when our passage speaks of the "Oral Torah," it does not mean the Talmud. Rather, it refers to the Human Torah, namely, the Written Torah as it relates to the material world. Why, then, is it called "oral"? Because, just as the Oral Torah acts as a "filter" that allows the Written Torah to be comprehended, so also the Human Torah acts as a filter that allows the Primordial Torah to be apprehended.

Thus, the Written Torah is to the Primordial Torah what the Oral Torah is to the Written Torah. In this sense, it could almost be said that the Written Torah is a higher aspect of the Oral Torah.

MOSHE AND RABBI AKIVA

The following passage of the Talmud can shed light on the concept of the hiddenness of the divine mind and the stages by which it is revealed to humanity.

When Moshe ascended to the heavenly realms to receive the Torah, he found the Holy One, Blessed be He, sitting there adding crowns to its letters.

He said to Him: "Master of the Universe, what is lacking in Your Torah [that You need to add these crowns]?"

God answered: "There is a man by the name of Akiva ben Joseph who will arise in the future. . . . He will know how to derive countless numbers of laws from each one of these crowns."

Moshe requested: "Master of the Universe, show him to me."

God replied: "Turn around."

So Moshe went and sat down in the eighth row of Rabbi Akiva's lecture hall. However, he did not understand even one word that was said there. Thereupon he fell into perplexity. Finally Rabbi Akiva's students asked their teacher:

"What is the source [of the law that you have just deduced from the crowns]"?

He said to them: "It is a law that was relayed to us by Moses at Sinai."

Upon hearing this Moses was comforted. He then returned to the Holy One, Blessed be He, and asked:

"Master of the Universe, since You have a man like this, why are You using me as Your messenger in giving the Torah?"

God replied: "Be silent, for this is the way I have determined it."

Moshe then made another request: "Master of the Universe, You have shown me this man's knowledge of the Torah. Now show me also his reward."

God told him: "Turn around."

He turned around and saw that Rabbi Akiva's torn flesh was being weighed at the market stalls. In astonishment he said:

"Master of the Universe, is this the Torah and is this its reward?"

God replied: "Be silent, for this is the way I have determined it."[22]

Apart from its extraordinary drama, there is a need to grasp the profound message concealed in this strange story. The narrative indicates that Rabbi Akiva could deduce laws from every crown, while Moshe could not. Students of the Talmud have often wondered if this implies that Rabbi Akiva somehow surpassed Moses in wisdom. In fact the Midrash seems to go even further. Moses could not understand Rabbi Akiva's talmudic discourses, while the students in the class could!

It is difficult to believe, however, that the Midrash means to imply such a lack in Moshe's wisdom, for it is well known that in order to achieve even the lowest level of prophecy one must already have achieved the highest level of humanly attainable understanding. Only then is one prepared to receive the higher divine knowledge that is granted to the prophet.[23]

It is clearly unnecessary to say that Moshe, the greatest of the prophets, was extraordinarily wise. A more careful investigation, based on our earlier observations, actually confirms Moshe's unsurpassed level of wisdom. It was explained earlier that the black fire engraved on white fire results in a Torah that is adapted to the human mind. It achieves this result because its letters, being a more physical contraction of the heavenly world of white fire, hide a great part of the white fire from our view. For the pure Primordial Torah is like the light of the sun. Just as the sun's rays can blind a person's unprotected eyes, so the white fire in its exalted form can blind his intellect. But if the sun's light is reduced by passing through a tinted lens, one can look at it. Similarly with the Torah. Only through the Torah in its "filtered" form, in which black letters hide white fire, may one see something of the Primordial Torah's sublime wisdom. The concealing of the Torah, then, is necessary for the revelation of its content.

The little black crowns attached to some of the Hebrew letters may therefore be seen as a further step in adapting the letters of the original Written Torah to the human level of understanding. The original black fire conceals the Primordial Torah, allowing for a human text composed of Hebrew letters. The Oral Torah further explains the Written Torah. In the same way, the crowns add an intermediate step of concealment, more than that offered by the Written Torah and less than that offered by the Oral Torah.

Moshe, because of his unusual wisdom, needed only that degree of concealment provided by the unembellished letters. This, together with the remaining white fire, allowed for a balanced situation under which he could master the Torah. But in Rabbi Akiva's days, many hundreds of years later, the intellectual capacity of the human mind had descended to a far lower level. For him, the remaining white fire did create a problem. It left too much revealed, and so it still blinded him. The text had, in other words, not yet "fallen" to his level. Therefore, an extra level of concealment had to be added to it so that he could receive it, and this was achieved by adding more "black fire," in the form of crowns.

God showed Moshe that throughout the many ages of Jewish history the process of concealment and humanization would need to continue in order that the continuously "falling" man would be able to maintain contact with the Torah. To make it intelligible for Rabbi Akiva's day, the crowns were incorporated on top of the letters of the Written Torah.

However, as we have seen, this process of humanization of the Torah is accomplished on different levels. For with the addition of the crowns to the letters, the physical form of the Torah stabilized. It had reached such a state that the development of the Oral Torah could "take over." The Sages' explanations and interpretations were able to continue the process of concealing and at the same time revealing the Torah to each generation according to the level at which it was capable of understanding.

Most of the mysteries of our midrash can now be clarified. The reason Moshe could not follow Rabbi Akiva's talmudic discourse was not his weak intellectual capacity but rather his unique and remarkable wisdom. Moses found it difficult to understand why Rabbi Akiva needed to use the crowns in his deduction of the various *halachot*. This world of interpretation was unknown to him since the black crowns were, for a man of his capacity, superfluous.

But then Rabbi Akiva, responding to an inquiry from his students, stated that the *halachah* that Rabbi Akiva connected with the crowns actually came as a tradition from Moshe. Only then did Moshe realize that Rabbi Akiva would have been unable to deal with these laws if the white fire had not been concealed by the crowns.

It follows that when Moshe went on to ask God, "Master of the Universe, since You have a man like this, why are You using me as Your messenger in giving the Torah?" he was reflecting his concern, not that he was not wise enough to understand the Torah, but that he might after all not be its best transmitter. He was afraid that his Torah knowledge was on such a supreme level that he would fail to communicate it even to his own contemporaries, let alone to future generations.

We can now understand God's strange response when Moshe doubted his suitability to be the bearer of the Torah—

which is the same response He gave when Moshe expressed his shock on seeing Rabbi Akiva's flesh being weighed in the market stalls: "Be silent, for this is the way I have determined it."

Even though Moshe did not need the black crowns, he still could not understand everything. In the last analysis he was part of a world in which concealment is a necessity. Human beings, even the most elevated and knowledgeable, cannot see the whole "divine picture." Just as the heavily tinted lenses required to gaze at the sun obscure a man's vision, so the black letters, while making it possible for man to catch a glimpse of the divine mind, also obscure his view of it.

Thus, even Moshe could not see what had been concealed by the black fire, and this is why God instructed Moshe to be silent. The answers to his questions were beyond his understanding. They had therefore been hidden by the black letters of the Torah. Only within God's private mind, the Primordial Torah, is there a justification for the ordeal of Rabbi Akiva and a solution to the mystery of why Moshe was preferred over him to become the intermediary between God and the People of Israel.

TORAH FOR OTHER WORLDS

From earlier conclusions, it is only one step toward a Torah in the world of souls. Jewish tradition tells us about an upper world from which the soul originates.[24] When the soul is slowly infused into the fetus after conception, it is still in contact with its transcendent realm, which is the sphere of the Primordial Torah. During the time preceding birth, the soul is immersed in learning this Torah, in a form appropriate to the unborn soul's spiritual level. All this while the soul is fully aware that once it enters the world, this Torah will be concealed from it to be replaced by the Human Torah. A moment before birth, the baby is severed from its connection with the "home base," and all this knowledge is forgotten.[25]

But in maturity, the person reencounters the Torah and subconsciously recognizes it to be the humanized form of the higher adaptation he had learned before he was born.

It has been suggested that this is the reason so many thousands of people are so deeply impressed by the contents of the Pentateuch and why this work has endured for so many generations: in it man recognizes the old code, the Primordial Torah of the other world. For man does not encounter the Torah for the first time while reading its pages but restudies the human edition of the ultimate Torah, which he had already encountered before he was born.

But this is not the end of the story, for the Jewish Sages tell us that a man's soul is not extinguished when his body passes away. At the end of his days he is called back to the upper world to meet the ultimate Torah again and to be rewarded for his study and fulfillment of the Human Torah in the lower world. This time he will sit among the righteous souls, who will all be crowned by the good deeds and Torah knowledge that they have earned. And this time he will again study Torah in a higher form that reflects the essence of God's mind.[26]

ADDENDUM

Does God observe His own commandments? This is a question that strikes us as preposterous. Still, it is a question that the Talmud asks in all sincerity![27] In a most unusual discussion, the Talmud contemplates the possibility of God wearing *tefillin* (phylacteries) or praying! Without hesitation the Sages answer in the affirmative.

This question is normally understood in terms of God's own morality: How can God ever command man to observe the *mitzvot* of the Torah when He Himself is not committed to these laws? How could a commander ever order his subjects if the commander himself failed to live up to his own rules?

There is, however, a deeper meaning to this inquiry. If the Torah (in its primordial form) is equal to God, then God Himself is the very "personification" of the Torah and consequently of the *mitzvot*. God then has to carry these *mitzvot* within Himself! This obviously does not mean that God observes the commandments as man does. In fact we may argue that God is the only One who *really* observes the commandments! The reasoning behind this is as follows.

Philosophers argue that "reality" in the highest sense of the word can only be established within God Himself. Nothing is more "real" than God. His existence is unconditional and infinite. Anything finite and physical is void compared to Him. In that sense, God is the only One who "really" exists. This may throw new light on different verses in the Torah that seem to speak about God in physical terms. For example, God takes the Jews out of Egypt with an "outstretched arm and a strong hand" (Deuteronomy 26:8). Maimonides and many others stress the metaphorical meaning of such expressions. There is, however, a different way of looking at such wording. One may argue that God "really" has hands. When one takes into account that "reality" means "infinite and unconditional" existence, it would be completely consistent to state that "real" hands happen to be spiritual "elements" within God. When looking, however, to a human hand, one might say that this is a poor and simplistic reflection of the "real" (i.e., spiritual) hand of God. The human hand, after all, is void and nothing when compared to God's hand.

In this sense human deeds, because they are finite, are not to be compared with the infinite actions of God. Only in God is there absolute reality, and consequently, only He can "perform" the *mitzvot* in the absolute and unqualified sense of the word.

When the Talmud suggests that God wears *tefillin* (phylacteries), it means that God wears *tefillin* in an infinite way. "Real" tefillin are metaphysical ideas to be found within God's mind. They are also represented in His attributes. When they are translated into man's terms, they will don human clothes and be represented by symbolic items such as the black phylacteries that Jews wear at their morning prayers.

In this sense, God performs the commandments. One could therefore argue that the *mitzvot* are divine attributes and that man and God have the *mitzvot* in common. This, however, leads to another important insight. In what we may call the greatest praise ever given to man, the Torah informs man that he was created in the image of God (Genesis 1:27). Keeping in mind the above observations, one may conclude that if man is indeed created in the image of God, then he is, ipso facto, also created in the image of the Torah and the *mitzvot*. Torah and God are, after all, one. The implication would be that man is inherently entrusted with the values of the Torah and the *mitzvot*. Being created in the image of God therefore means being born from the values of the Torah. From his birth, man carries the Torah within him, since it is the "material" from which he is made.

It has often been said that man is not in need of the *Aseret Ha-Dibrot* (the "Ten Sayings," erroneously rendered as "Ten Commandments"). Somehow, man carries the values of these commandments within his heart. They are seen as his intuition, guilty conscience, or "categorical imperative." Consequently, he does not need to be told about them. While one could no doubt argue that so much evil in this world proves that many have never heard of these imperatives, it could, however, be said that Judaism basically agrees with the notion that man *does* carry these commandments in his heart. *The Torah is carried within the human heart.* The question, however, is whether or not he will harken to its voice.

The suggestion that we can do without the Ten Sayings is therefore faulty. While man carries the Torah within his heart, *he will still be in need of an external Torah*, the Pentateuch and its commentaries, to *remind* him of the Torah that he carries in his heart. As a moral being, man is capable of being deaf to his own inner voice, the inner Torah. Too many layers of unnatural substance block the way to his real "I." While this is the price he pays for the exercise of freedom of will, it also happens to be his greatest privilege. Freedom of will is what makes man a human being and, as such, different from the animal world.

This leads to a most interesting observation. Man's basic nature is to live by the commandments. They are his inherent disposition. He is fashioned from these values. Seen in this light, one may argue that it is not only those *mitzvot* normally called the rational laws (*sichliyot*) that are inborn but also those that cannot be understood easily (*shemiyot*) are somehow implanted within the deepest consciousness of man.

For many human beings, to be free means to do as they please, without restriction. While this author would have to object that this is an oversimplistic and even dangerous attitude, there is, however, a certain truth to this: When man lives in accordance with his own nature, that is, his inner voice, which is the voice of the Torah, he has indeed found freedom. He does what he would like to do: to be himself, to live by the imperatives of the Torah.

For man to be free is to live in the ways of the Torah. This is the deeper meaning behind the Sages' statement, "Who is free? He who busies himself with the Torah."[28]

There is, however, still another implication. If freedom is to be found by those who occupy themselves with the Torah, then freedom is not to be found by those who do not live within the spirit and imperatives of the Torah. Freedom is only the privilege of those who live a life of Torah. This implication follows from the earlier observations. Freedom is the result of listening to one's inner voice, the Torah. Consequently, violation of the Torah is the result of listening to a "foreign" voice, a voice that obscures the truth of one's inner "I." Instead of arguing that those who live in accordance with the Torah are restricted and lack the joy of real freedom, the conclusion must be that those who do not live within the spirit of the Torah are the ones who are constrained. Instead of being master over their desires, their passions master them. This is not freedom.

8

On *Halachah* as
the Art of Amazement

n the way that man observes the world and interacts with it, he reveals one of the most surprising and impressive sides to all of human existence: the faculty of appreciation. When walking through a landscape he can be overwhelmed by its beauty. Wondering at the sky, standing at the seashore, or viewing the sunset, he becomes aware of an inner, uplifting experience that he cannot verbalize. Enjoying the music of Mozart, Beethoven, or Paganini, man can be lifted to unprecedented heights. Through the constant search for beauty, harmony, conformity, and so forth, man confirms his unique place in this universe.

But even in the "small moments" of man's life, he shows an unusual appreciation for his surroundings. When choosing the interior of his home or the color and style of his clothes, he will carefully select colors, patterns, and specific combinations. Many hours, if not days and months (or years), are spent on this endeavor. For most people this is far from a waste of time but rather a deep emotional need that enriches their lives.

Things must "go well," flow into each other, and create a picture of great harmony, tranquillity, and beauty. One blotch of paint will not inspire us, but a certain combination of them definitely does. One musical note is boring, but the flowing of many of them within a certain pattern will make a symphony that can bring thousands of listeners to exaltation.

Art collectors will pay large amounts of money to become the owners of paintings that are often no larger than a few square centimeters. Some paintings are valued at millions of dollars and are viewed by hundreds of thousands of human beings, who are often prepared to travel long distances to view them. The world of haute couture has, for thousands of years, produced an infinite amount of elegant (and not so elegant) garments of all kinds and fashions. Instead of man tiring of all these efforts and getting bored, he is deeply involved in all this, searching for every possible new way to make sure that beauty and novelty will always be with him.

HOW DID WE GET LIKE THAT?

Let us ask: How did we get like that? Rudolf Otto and many others have already made us realize that we cannot adequately explain why we enjoy music or fall in love with a painting or the seashore.[1]

Indeed, what is there about beauty that makes it beautiful? What is there so great about a van Gogh, or the music of Beethoven? Is there not a certain absurdity to all this? How is it that we can hear more than one musical note at a time? And why is it that we do not just hear the different notes together but also apprehend them as a unity? We somehow grasp them. We are conscious of the music and its beauty. There is indeed a faculty called appreciation. But what is this faculty made of?

The American philosopher G. N. M. Tyrrel (in his *Grades of Significance*), writing about "reading," reminds the reader of this most miraculous faculty of man:[2]

> A book we will suppose, has fallen into the hands of intelligent beings who know nothing of what writing and printing mean, but they are accustomed to dealing with the external relationships of things. They try to find out the laws of the book, which for them mean the principles governing the order in which the letters are arranged. . . . [T]hey will think they have discovered the laws of the book when they formulated certain rules governing the external relationships of the letters. That each word and each sentence expresses a meaning will never dawn on them because their background of thought is made up of concepts which deal only with external relationships, and explanations to them means solving the puzzle of these external relationships. . . . Their methods will never reach the grade of significance which contains the idea of meanings.

Why do we associate sounds with meaning? How is it that meaningless shapes are capable of triggering within us the concept of meaning?

Perhaps the most outstanding example of man's mysterious nature is the experience of love. If we could imagine a creature from outer space looking at the human body, what would he see? Probably one of the most repulsive creations walking around in the cosmos. "Deformed" organs such as protrusions of flesh hanging on both sides of some kind of roundness or enlarged balloon on top of the human body. In the middle of this ball, called a head, there is another extension placed between two items of glass, and below, a hole into which man disposes of all sorts of substances (which by outer space standards have a most offensive taste!). Legs and arms will be described in most uncomplimentary terms. Most astonishing of all would no doubt be the fact that these "monstrous" creations fall in love with each other, fight wars because of jealousy, and like to have intimate relationships that result in producing even more of these unsightly creatures.

Why, indeed, do we not consider music an abhorrent experience, a Rembrandt painting the ravings of a hideous human creativity, or lovemaking as a most repulsive act?

AMAZEMENT

This, in fact, touches on the very core of religion and the problem of secularism. Western civilization has a very specific approach to life. It is highly pragmatic. Matters are basically seen from a purely utilitarian point of view. Everything is measured by result-getting standards. What matters is whether things "work." Humans have become toolmaking creatures for whom the world is a gigantic toolbox for the satisfaction of their needs. Satisfaction, luxury, and pleasure are man's goals. Everything is calculated, and there is supreme faith in statistics.

This has possibly caused the greatest problem of our times: the tragedy of existential indifference, missing out on *exactly* that which is no doubt the most exciting side of life—the mysterium tremendum that lies behind all existence, after every move man makes, behind every human experience. It is the invisible part of life where the real flow of life runs, that which the five senses cannot grasp or touch. Modern man takes notice of what surrounds him and tells himself that everything will be explained. Man looks to the skeleton but does not see the content and the essence.

Maurice Nicoll describes this very well when he discusses the fact that humans cannot even see themselves or their fellowmen:[3]

> We can all see another person's body directly. We see the lips moving, the eyes opening and shutting, the lines of the mouth and face changing, and the body expressing itself as a whole in action. The person *himself* is invisible. . . . If the invisible side of people were discerned as easily as the visible side we would live in a *new humanity*. As we are we live in visible humanity, a humanity of appearances. . . . All our thoughts, emotions, feelings, imaginations, reveries, dreams, fantasies are *invisible*. All that belongs to our scheming, planning secrets, ambitions, all our hopes, fears, doubts, perplexities, all our affections, speculations, ponderings, vacuities, uncertainties, all our desires, longings, appetites, sensations, our likes, dislikes, aversions, attractions, loves and hates—all are themselves invisible. They constitute "one's self." (italics added)

Nicoll insists that while all this may *appear* obvious, it is not at all overt:

> It is an extremely difficult thing to grasp. . . . We do not grasp that we are invisible. We do not realize that we are in a world of invisible people. We do not understand that *life before all other definitions of it, is a drama of the visible and the invisible.*[4] (italics added)

When I buy grain, my main interest is that it is alive and not dead. But that life I cannot see, touch, or smell. An unconscious cat, even though still alive, is not a real cat until it regains consciousness. This is what philosophers call "inner space." The matter itself is, however, mysterious. "Analyze, weigh and measure a tree as you please, observe its form and function, its genesis and the laws to which it is subject, still an acquaintance with its essence never comes about."[5]

What smites us with total amazement is *not* what we grasp and are able to convey, but that what lies within our reach is beyond our grasp—not the quantitative aspect of nature, but something qualitative. Everything is more than the sum total of its parts. Man is aware of it, but it is beyond description or comprehension.

Even the very act of thinking baffles thinking: the most incomprehensible fact is that man can comprehend altogether! That which man can apprehend man cannot comprehend. That which man takes account of, cannot be accounted for! "The search of reason ends at the shore of the known. We sail because our mind is like a fantastic seashell and when applying our ear to its lips, we hear a perpetual murmur from the wave beyond the shore."[6] And only through the awareness of this mystery does man start to live. Only then can he experience what real life is all about. The beginning of happiness lies in the understanding that life without the awareness of mystery is not worth living. Why? Because all life really starts in wonder and amazement! Being struck by the impenetrable mysterium of all being, the soul becomes reawakened. As if struck by fire, man is taken by a radical amazement.

This is the beginning of all genuine religion. Because of man's astonishment with the world and himself, he recognizes the masterly hand of God. He ponders over the grandeur and sublimity of God. When seeing God as the foundation of all mystery, he starts to feel Him in his bones, in all that he does, feels, thinks and says!

As has been said, the tendency to take everything for granted and the indifference to the sublime is the root of all irreligiosity. It is a way toward the secularization of the world. *Religion is a protest against taking things for granted.* It is the art of living in amazement.

HALACHAH

To be aware of the total mystery of all matter, to feel it, to breathe it, is obviously not an easy task. To become aware of the great secret behind all being is no doubt an art. How does man capture the notion of wonder and amazement and inject this into his very life? Some people sense these qualities at distant intervals, in extraordinary events, but can one capture it in every moment?

This, the author would suggest, is only possible by capturing the mysterium and transforming it into a *way of living.* This is the purpose of the *halachah*: to experience the mysterium in and through commonplace deeds. *Halachah* is the art of revealing the nonhuman side, the metahuman side, the divine dimension through the medium of every human act. *Halachah* is there to teach us that our humanity is utterly inexplicable, that man should stand trembling before God.

Judaism teaches that proper deeds lead to correct and true thinking. Deeds create mentality: the actual deed of killing creates a mentality to kill, the distribution of charity creates a mind-set to care for one's fellowman. Likewise, certain deeds have the power of making man walk through life in the awareness of the mysterium behind all human existence.

By giving deeds a certain direction, they become sensitized to the notion of mystery. By living *halachah* we hold back and allow for a moment of reflection. It creates a mind-set not to take anything for granted but to become amazed by the very deed that follows. The dietary laws make man take notice, while eating, of the very wondrous existence of food, by making a *brachah* (blessing) on the miracle of eating. It stalls a deed, giving it an opportunity to transcend being a commonplace act and to become a higher deed. It causes a new profound reflection on life. Consequently, it provides for a different and more dignified way of living. It makes man take notice of his deeds and his life and ask, Why am I acting? What is the meaning of a human act and, therefore, of life?

What is there in the human *deed* that it should be the main carrier of this message? Is action the most important manifestation of human life? Why is philosophical reflection without the deed not good enough? Did not the Greeks contemplate the mystery of life without the *halachah*? Does one really have to act so as to know?

It is in the deed that man meets himself. In deeds man becomes aware of what his life is really all about: the power to harm, to wreck, and to destroy, but also the possibility of deriving joy and bestowing it upon others, of relieving or intensifying one's own and other people's tension. The deed shows man who he really is and not what he would like to be. Here his own self is exposed: what man does not dare to think, he shows in his deeds. The "real" heart of man is revealed in his deeds. Man may have lofty ideas but behave like a criminal. History teaches that noble ideas are no guarantee for noble deeds. And since God provided man with a world in which noble deeds are by far the most powerful ways to build and fashion this world, it is the deed that counts. No noble thought ever changed this world for the better if it did not become a noble deed. Metaphysics is not known for giving birth to noble deeds.

But even when philosophical speculation would conduce man to act nobly, it would slowly evaporate into thin air if it did not go hand in hand with a firm and continuous commitment to a pragmatic deed. It is the deed that upholds the thought.

It should be added that such an approach will only bear fruit when these deeds are constantly repeated. No human deed will leave its mark if done only once. To become effective it must grow into some kind of a habit as the result of its having rooted itself in the deep consciousness of man. Things continually done come to be done subconsciously. "Could the young but realize how soon they will become mere walking bundles of habits, they would give more heed to their conduct while in the plastic state. We are spinning our own fates, good or evil and never to be undone."[7]

Habit is capitalized action. Habit becomes conscience. For this reason alone Judaism sees the deed as the key to teach man to recognize the mysterium. By way of rituals, blessings, and so on, often done in a habitual way and becoming second nature, man will subconsciously open himself up to the experience of amazement. *Obviously this is no guarantee.* Deeds, even when they carry the potential to reveal the mysterium, do not automatically result in a greater awareness. This will always depend on man's "conscious" awareness of what he is doing. Only when man wills it to happen will the subconscious mind activate this potentiality. What it does, however, is to lay the subconscious foundation of this awareness, so that if man should wish to capitalize on it, he may—thus enabling him to realize the wondrous aspect of human existence.

In other words, a halachic life is *not* a guarantee that one will become consciously aware of the need to be amazed. One can live a halachic life without any notion of amazement. But what is important is that the *halachah* gives man the option so that if he *wants*, he can achieve amazement, since he plants in his subconscious the seed for amazement. He turns his subconscious mind into an instrument that will take notice of the mysterium.

It is also the uniqueness of "time" of which *halachah* makes man aware. It is in time that man meets God. Every second that passes by is never to return. This makes time extremely precious. Consequently, it must be handled with the greatest of care. It teaches man that there are no insignificant moments or deeds. Whatever is done by man is to be done within the framework of an encounter with God. This requires that every deed be done with the awareness that one stands before the Lord of the universe and that every little matter, however unimportant in the eyes of man, counts. It is done in the presence of the King!

A NEW AWARENESS

The aim is to infuse purely subjective emotions, needs, and desires with a new awareness—one that otherwise is almost congenitally foreign to the entire component of the human personality. The religious system of Judaism, which disciplines the Jew in every situation all through life, establishes habitual patterns of bodily reaction and conduct that testify to an acute awareness of an order of reality that is not of the body. In that sense it liberates man from taking things for granted. This liberating act is a *means*, *not* a guarantee that it will result in a higher consciousness of amazement.

When a Jew is overcome with nausea at the sight of

nonkosher food, such a reaction is not natural; it is not in keeping with the laws of normal human experience. The reaction shows the awareness of some *outside will* that his personality has acquired. In a sense, the nausea reflects the partial transformation of the natural desire for food into the desire for that which is beyond man.

It has often been said that *halachah* requires mechanical, ritual performances. What is more important, the conscious worship of the mind or the quasi-automatic performances of the body? This is a question based on an utterly mistaken conception of the human personality. Man is made of body and soul. The body cannot worship consciously, and the mind is incapable of serving by way of ritual. Man is not only body or soul; he is the result of both and therefore in need of serving God in a way that corresponds to the body as well as to the soul, each according to its own nature. On the level of the soul, the relationship to God is spiritual and conscious, but there is no place for action. On the level of the body, there is no place for "conscious" worship. It can only be materialized into action. Only a combination can lead to an appropriate result. In the deed, the *mitzvah* is the union of the two. The *mitzvah* is never only thought, nor is it a mere reflex action. The *mitzvah* is a deed that is of the spirit and of the body at the same time. The subconscious condition toward the will of God and the mysterium tremendum is brought about by continuous conscious suggestion.

Halachah is designed to make our lives compatible with our sense of the mysterium. What counts is not if it is compatible with common sense or the "obvious," but with that which is unspoken. What it wants to accomplish is to bring together the passing with the everlasting, the momentary with the eternal. And only through the human deed, transformed into a *mitzvah*, will it accomplish that task—to bring eternity into man's life, to redeem God's power in every human experience, to discover divinity within man himself. Once it has done so, it is capable of turning every human deed into a *mitzvah*.

TO DESERVE

The fact that man is capable of acting, building, investigating, enjoying, and being aware that he can only take account of these faculties, but not account for them, confronts him with another inescapable question: Does he *deserve* these faculties? No normal man is without some concern for truth, beauty, or love. But can he make any claim on them? The shattering truth is that man does not deserve them, that he could not possibly deserve them. Nobody ever earned the right to love, to enjoy. No one ever earned these faculties through his or her talents or abilities. They are gifts, not rewards earned. It is as simple as that! Man experiences thousands of things and not one of them is really earned. This is most embarrassing! Man eats from Somebody's table without taking notice.

Man's first concern should therefore be, Am I worthy? Do I deserve all this? How can I make myself worthy of all this? How will man respond to all these undeserved gifts? Without response there is no dignity! Love obligates, man must respond! Man needs to *discharge* his debts toward God. Only through that will he attain dignity.

This is another aspect of halachic life. By living in accordance with *halachah* as discussed above, man responds to God's ultimate gifts. He recognizes God's fingerprint in every and any matter. By redeeming God's power in this world, man sanctifies all his deeds; man becomes worthy of life!

Love becomes law in the life of the beloved. To be aware that man is the recipient of genuine love he imposes upon himself disciplines—the dos and the donts—that make him worthy of this love. This is, in fact, the hallmark of the mature human being. God's love becomes God's commandment. Moral consequences follow, not without struggle and difficulties, not without the constant need to revise and rethink. With hard work, the heavens open and this awareness of the mystery becomes man's experience.

9

On Milk and Meat

o doubt, there is one law within the Jewish tradition that has puzzled many Jewish scholars.
This is the law that prevents the Jew from mixing milk with meat. Its source is found in the
Torah (Exodus 23:19; 34:26, Deuteronomy
14:21), but no clue is provided as to its meaning.

Strangely enough, it is this mysterious law that has had
the greatest influence on the daily life of Jews for thousands
of years, right up to this very day. It divides the Jewish kitchen
into two parts, a meat and milk section, and makes it necessary to have two sets of pots, pans, forks, and knives. This
law hovers over much of Jewish life and has turned it into
something very distinctive.

What could be the reason behind this law? While it may
be argued that many other Jewish dietary laws try to infuse
man with a sense of human sensitivity, this can hardly be said
about the law of milk and meat. It could, for example, be argued that those animals or fowls that are forbidden are forbidden because they are carnivorous, kill, and are aggressive,
and it is the will of the Torah that man should distance him-

self from such traits. But the mixture of milk and meat does not seem to accentuate any particular unwanted characteristic.

There is, however, another strange dimension to this law. It is not only forbidden to consume a mixture of milk and meat but the *very blending* (in the form of cooking, baking, etc.) of these components is also forbidden, even when they are not to be consumed![1] One is obliged to destroy this mixture. This reminds us of the law of the Passover festival, which not only forbids the consumption of leavened bread (*chametz*) but even forbids having it in one's possession.[2] But while one could still sell the leavened bread, this is not possible in the case of a mixture of milk and meat. The obligation to destroy this mixture of milk and meat seems, therefore, to indicate a most acute matter that does not allow for any compromise. Why should this be the case?

KABBALAH

Kabbalistic tradition has it that God created the world with the specific purpose for man to sanctify it. Man is asked to infuse the world with the divine spark that is found within himself since he was created in the image of God (Genesis 1:27).

To make the creation of the universe possible, God had to "withdraw" His *En Sof*, His infinite spiritual light. Only in this "void" or "darkness" would physical existence become possible. This principle is called *tzimtzum* (self-limitation) and is one of the most difficult concepts to understand within the entire kabbalistic philosophy.

Once man was created, God told man that it was his task to make sure that this "withdrawn" light would (at least partially) return. This would be possible through the means of "sanctification." By connecting all physical elements with the *En Sof*, this withdrawn light would return and the universe would be lifted from its purely physical dimensions. This was to be done through the fulfillment of the commandments and the study of Torah, which would make man see the fingerprint of God in all existence. Ultimately, everything should revert back to God, the Infinite Source.[3]

One way through which one could grasp this concept is to imagine a circle that is open on top. The open space on top is the initial point of creation. The circle itself symbolizes the way through which the world has to "journey" until it will, on completing the circle, reenter the initial open space on top of the circle—the infinite world.

The circle has, however, another important feature as well. It also symbolizes the *limits* in the confines within which the world must travel to return to its original Source (symbolized by the open space on top of the circle). As long as the world moves along and *within* the line of the circle, it will finally be connected with the original Source. But if it broke *through* this circle, then it would "run wild," no longer able to bring itself back into the confines of the circle. As such, it would *not* revert back to the original Source, and consequently, would fail to fulfill its purpose. This would mean devastation and chaos.

The line of the circle itself must also be seen as the symbol of the "dividing line" between that which is "permitted" and that which is "forbidden." Everything *inside* the circle is ensured of its possibility to return to its Source and, as such, is "permissible." There is still a connection with the Source, regardless of how far something may be removed from the original Source (symbolized by the open space on top). Consequently, the dividing line is the border between that which is "permitted" (inside) and that which is "forbidden" (outside).

For this reason, kabbalistic thought teaches that what is

more material and therefore "independent" lies closer to the outside (i.e., borderline) of the circle. All that which is less "material" and more dependent on God is more to the center of the circle and, as such, less removed from its original Source.

When looking in the Creation chapter, we find that a certain evolving process took place which made the animal world appear at the end of the "six days" of the Creation, just before the appearance of man. (Genesis 1:25). This evolving process reveals a constant increase in "independence"— greater mobility and physicality. While the plants are still completely dependent on the Divine Source, having no "say" of their own, the small insects and creatures are more autonomous. This independence increases most drastically with the creation of the larger animals on the sixth day.

THE ANIMAL WORLD

As such, the superior animal must be seen as the most autonomous creature within the corporeal world. *Unlike* man, the animal is not blessed with a divine soul and has no part in a spiritual, moral existence. The animal is completely bound by the physical world in the sense that it cannot "rise" above the laws of nature. In this sense it is the *most* developed physical creature within the world. Consequently, it is the animal that walks on the borderline of our circle.

This has far-reaching consequences. Since the animal has developed to the outermost borderline of the circle, it treads a most dangerous path: one more step and it will find itself *outside* the borderline. As such, it will become "over-developed," "running wild" and losing its connection with the Source on top of the circle. This must be prevented at all costs, since it would lead to chaos. In other words, this animal is never, through overdevelopment, to become a "super-animal." It is not allowed to become more physical than it already is. To emphasize the point, it could be argued that animal flesh is not to become superflesh, developing beyond the limits of the borderline of the circle.

MILK

What is milk? Milk is, no doubt, the most important nutrient for the development of the human and animal body. It is nourishment par excellence. It contains all the ingredients that enable proper physical development.

The reader may now begin to understand the "danger" of mixing milk with meat. The animal is the most advanced of all physical existence. It finds itself on the borderline of the circle. Any addition to its physicality will force it out of the circle. It will sever its connection with the Source and become "overdeveloped," creating "superflesh."

Since milk is the very substance by which the body develops, it would be a fatal mistake to "add" this nutrient to "fully developed" meat. The milk would continue to develop the meat beyond its proper borders. This would purport a wish to "overdevelop" the already optimally developed "flesh" of the animal. It would be as if one wanted to make the animal world break out of the circle and sever its connection with its Source. This would mean the denial of the very purpose of this world.

This explains the ruling that one is not only forbidden to consume such a mixture but also is obliged to destroy this mixture even when one does not intend to consume it. Its very existence is a denial of the foundation of God's plan with His creation.

10

On Bible Criticism and Its Counterarguments

A SHORT HISTORY[1]

One of traditional Judaism's most important claims is its total commitment to the divinity of the text of the Torah, the Pentateuch. It is believed that the other books of *Tanach* may contain a human element since "no two prophets prophesied in the same style."[2] But the Torah came to Moshe from God in a manner that is metaphorically called "speaking," after which Moshe wrote it down "like a scribe writing from dictation."[3]

In the nineteenth century, this belief came under severe attack by a theory called Higher Criticism or *Quellenscheidung*. This theory denied the divinity of the Torah as a verbal account of God's words to Moshe. Instead, the text was seen to be made up of a conglomeration of various sources compiled over many hundreds of years. As such, it could not have been written by Moshe.[4]

The proponent of this theory was Julius Wellhausen (1844-1918), a German Semitic scholar and professor of theology and oriental studies. Wellhausen, however, was not the first to doubt the "authenticity" of the Torah. In the seventeenth century, the famous Dutch philosopher Benedictus de Spinoza (1632-1677), who was a descendant of the Marranos, stated in his *Tractatus Theologico-Politicus* (and in some letters) that he doubted the Mosaic and the divine authorship of the Torah.[5]

Spinoza's major point was that the Bible, like many other literary works, should be seen as the product of human spiritual development, mostly of a primitive nature. While accepting the possibility that some parts of the Torah could have originated with Moshe, he contended that it was only many centuries after Moshe died that the Torah, as we know it today, appeared. Ezra the Scribe (fourth century B.C.E.) should be considered the major author and editor of the Torah as well as of the Books of Joshua, Judges, Samuel, and Kings. Because Ezra died prematurely, these works were never revised and are therefore full of contradictions and repetitions.

Because Spinoza never reached any systematic or clear conclusion, Jean Astruc (1684-1766), a French physician, is considered the real founder of classical Bible Criticism. Being a conservative, Astruc concluded in his work (published anonymously in Brussels and Paris, 1753), *Conjectures sur les memoires originaux, dont il parait que Moses s'est servi pour composer le livre de la Genese,* that Moshe, the redactor of Genesis and the first two chapters of Exodus, made use of two parallel sources and ten fragments written before his time. These primary sources refer to God as *Y-H-V-H* and *Elohim*, respectively.

Although Astruc's conclusion aroused intense opposition, scholars like J. G. Einhorn (1752-1827) attached much importance to his work. It was Julius Wellhausen, however, who gave full impetus to this theory, and his name is identified with the Graf-Wellhausen Hypothesis or Documentary Theory.[6]

Wellhausen wanted to prove that the Torah and the Book of Joshua were, in large measure, "doctored" by priestly canonizers under Ezra in the time of the Second Temple. Their purpose was to perpetuate a single falsehood: Moshe's authorship of the Torah and the central worship, first in the Tabernacle and later in the Temple. According to Wellhausen, there never was a Tabernacle and no revelation at Sinai ever took place. Moshe, if he ever existed, considered the Deity a local thunder god or mountain god. The Torah had, therefore, to be seen as a complete forgery and not as a verbal account of God's words to Moshe and the People Israel.

In 1875, Wellhausen published his *Prolegomena to the History of Ancient Israel*, an unusual work with almost five thousand textual references covering the whole of the Old Testament. In this work, Wellhausen purports to present the *true* biblical story. Relying heavily on his forerunners, he maintained that four major documents could be identified in the Torah. Each had an individual character, both in content and in general outlook. Though they had been skillfully interwoven, their special characteristics made it possible to trace each source throughout the books of the Torah. The earliest was the *-J- Document* (J being the first letter of the Divine Name, which was used throughout this source and so became essential). It was followed soon after by the *Elohist Document -E-*, in which God is designated as Elohim. These documents were thought to have been composed in the early monarchical period, probably in the ninth or eighth century B.C.E.

The Book of Deuteronomy -D-, which gave a narrative framework to the "Book of the Law," promulgated by King Yoshia in the seventh century B.C.E., was primarily a code of law based on prophetic principles.

The Priestly Code (P), a universal history and extensive legal code, was chiefly concerned with matters of cult and was dominated by the priestly interest in prescribing the correct ritual for each ceremonial occasion. K. H. Graf had already assigned it to the post-exilic age and connected it with the Law of Ezra in the fifth century B.C.E.

Wellhausen's method is clear and straightforward. Every passage that fits his theory is authentic; all others are forgeries. Whenever possible, he points out poor grammar, corrupt vocabulary, and alleged internal inconsistencies. In cases where he felt some "need" to change the plain meaning of a Hebrew word to fit into this theory, he offered what he called "conjectural emendation." The fact that thousands of verses contradicted his theory never disturbed Wellhausen. He contended that there was a master forger or interpolator at work who anticipated Wellhausen's theory and consequently inserted passages and changed verses so as to refute it. Wellhausen assumed that the forger had worked, as it were, with scissors and paste, taking all kinds of liberties: carving up the original texts; moving half a sentence here, a few sentences down, and three and a half sentences there, and a few sentences up, while altogether suppressing and omitting large portions of each source that could not be fitted into this patchwork. He claimed to be more clever than the interpolator could have ever imagined and therefore to have divulged the real truth. This obviously was a wonderful theory, for arguments against Wellhausen's theory thereby became his strongest defenders!

With the publication of this masterpiece, Wellhausen introduced a new era in the world of Bible studies, and most of his contemporaries, as well as their students, accepted his conclusions as gospel. His influence on younger scholars was profound and far-reaching. For a full generation, he dominated Old Testament scholarship, not only in his own country but also in England[7] and America.[8]

The most important histories of Israel and of Hebrew literature, as well as a host of commentaries and introductions, were based more or less directly on the Wellhausen system. The commentaries edited by Wilhelm Nowack and Karl Marti,[9] as well as those of the *International Critical Commentary on the Holy Scriptures*, were indebted to Wellhausen's theories.[10]

His students continued to use his method and discovered within their teacher's *J, E, P,* and *D* documents at least thirty additional documents. Each document (especially *J* and *E*) contained a number of older elements; each had undergone a certain amount of "editorial" revision in an effort to coordinate and harmonize the various elements within the style of the original. The additional materials were so extensive that they could not have been the products of only a handful of authors, but rather belonged to a complete religious school.[11]

The materials were cut even finer. Slowly, more and more forgeries were "discovered," until finally half a dozen documents were found for each single verse, and others even went as far as tracing them through some of the other books of *Tanach* as well. The whole theory degenerated into a reductio ad absurdum. Already in his own day, objective and honest scholars raised objections against Wellhausen's incredible guesswork and fantasies. The chancellor of England, the earl of Halsbury, referred to it in 1915 as "great rubbish."[12] The famous historian Lecky sharply criticized it on the basis that it totally lacked evidence.[13]

In 1908 Wellhausen came under heavy attack by B. D. Eerdmans,[14] while in 1925, Professor Rudolf Kittel, originally an admirer of Wellhausen's theories, stated that "the assumption of forgery may be one of those hypotheses which, once set up, is so often repeated that finally everyone believes it. Who nowadays would take upon himself the odium of being 'behind the times'?"[15]

Among the generations of critics who came to maturity after World War I, new insights provided by later approaches to *Tanach* made the Higher Criticism of the preceding generation seem less than adequate. Slowly it appeared to the scholars that new criteria had to be established and that historical criticism had its limitations. Hugo Gressmann declared that "in our field we need not more but less literary-critical research. The Higher Criticism has generally exhausted the problems which it could and had to solve."[16]

Scholars began ascribing the books of the Torah and the rest of *Nach* to earlier periods and stated that the legal principles of the Torah were already well established in the time of the prophet Samuel.[17] This tendency to regard much of the narrative and law in the Torah as more ancient brought into question what had once been accepted as the assured result of criticism.

The dating of Deuteronomy has always been the central point from which the critics had worked forward and backward to determine the age of the other law codes and documents. The description of Deuteronomy as the immediate inspiration for the reform and centralization of the "cultus" had been the starting point for Wellhausen's reconstruction of the religious history of Israel. With the dating of Deuteronomy, the whole critical edifice stood or fell.

Adam C. Welsh's earlier dating was, therefore, a major blow to the whole critical school and consequently not easily accepted by his contemporaries.[18] His view was, however, strengthened a decade later by certain conclusions of Otto

Eissfeldt regarding the nature and history of the Pentateuchal law.[19]

While the origin of much of the law was being moved back in time, the alternative that the final dates of the law codes should be moved down, was also considered. While Gustav Holscher dated Deuteronomy later than had the Wellhausen school, most scholars were of the opinion that earlier dates were more plausible.[20] It became increasingly clear that Wellhausen's theory of the history of Judaism was inadequate.

This does not suggest that the scholars agreed, for different dates were suggested and new theories contradicting each other were published. What became clear was that Bible Criticism was developing into a chaos of conflicting conjectures producing contradictory results and generating the impression that this type of research was ineffective.[21]

Moreover, in Jewish circles, sharp protest was raised. Although these theories did not impress the greatest Jewish scholars, they highly influenced many assimilated Jewish communities (especially in Germany). The Reform movement, perhaps searching for a means to support its objections against observance, embraced this theory and contributed some of its strongest proponents. Rabbi Samson Raphael Hirsch (1808-1888), in his Torah Commentary,[22] Dr. David Hoffmann (1843-1921),[23] an Orthodox Jewish scholar of great erudition, and Professor Jacob Barth (1851-1914),[24] another outstanding philologist of his time, destroyed much of Wellhausen's theory. Also, Rabbi Yitzchak Isaac Halevi (1847-1914), in his historical works, showed the position of Wellhausen and his admirers to be untenable.[25] In non-Orthodox Jewish circles, Wellhausen also came under sharp attack. One of the most profound analyses in this field was written by Benno Jacob (1862-1945) in his book on Genesis, *Das Erste Buch der Torah,* which concludes (p. 1048) with the words, "The theory that the Book of Genesis is composed of various sources that can be singled out and separated has been rejected."

Later non-Orthodox scholars, in particular Umberto Cassuto (1883-1951)[26] and Yechiel Kaufman (1889-1963)[27] further demolished the theory, showing that Wellhausen's observations contradicted his conclusions. Kaufman's main contribution lies in his thesis that monotheism was not, as Wellhausen and others had stated, a gradual departure from paganism, but an entirely new development. Israel's monotheism began with Moshe and was a complete revolution in religious thought.

Why were these earlier-mentioned theories ever accepted? In Wellhausen's day the theory of evolution was dominant. Darwin had won the day, and any discipline, including literature, that accepted the theory of evolution was welcomed with open arms. Furthermore, the philosopher Hegel (1770-1831) had left a deep impression in German and European culture by contending that all of history is a development from lower to progressively higher stages. It was therefore assumed that the Jewish religion developed from idolatry, and having passed through many intermediate stages, the earlier one of which was the Torah, reached the ultimate pure monotheism of latter days.

Special mention should be made of the famous archaeologist William F. Albright.[28] He convincingly demonstrated that archaeological research did not support, and in fact often contradicted, this view of history. In many of his works, Albright destroyed the very foundations upon which Wellhausen's edifice had been erected.

In retrospect, it is rather surprising that Wellhausen's

theories were accepted for so long. How is it possible that so many scholars promulgated similar theories and totally ignored or attacked those who differed?[29] Albright and others have pointed out that besides Hegelian theories, other motivations kept the Wellhausen tradition alive. Christian scholars were eager to attribute greater significance to the New Testament than the Old. In order to make this plausible, it had to be proven that large portions of the Torah were falsified and were not to be taken seriously.

When anti-Semitic tendencies became stronger in the immediate pre-Hitler days, many scholars felt the need to use the Wellhausen and other theories to give a final blow to the Jewish People, religion, and Bible. When Friedrich Delitzch (1850–1922) delivered a lecture called "Babel und Bibel," in which *Tanach* was considered devoid of any religious or moral value, Kaiser Wilhelm congratulated him for helping "to dissipate the nimbus of the Chosen People."[30]

The Germans, convinced of their status as *Herrenvolk* suffered from Teutomania and believed that anything must either be German or valueless, according to William F. Albright. Solomon Schechter, who headed the Jewish Theological Seminary in its earlier and more Orthodox days, exclaimed that Higher Criticism was no more than higher anti-Semitism. Albright asked the question, how was it possible that the "scientific community" accepted many of these theories without critical assessment, knowing that many of the scholars had shown that their personal anti-Semitism completely overshadowed their intellectual honesty.[31]

While Wellhausen and other schools of Higher Criticism slowly lost their credibility, a new school developed, introducing the anthropological approach. It saw religion as a general feature of the cultural history of mankind and made it possible to view Torah (and the rest of the *Tanach*) in the broad light of the universal experience of humanity. The anthropological approach to the study of religion was first applied to the whole of *Tanach* by William Robertson Smith.[32]

The general trend of Smith's interpretation was determined by the view, common to anthropologists, that religion was an integral part of life, not to be treated as an entity separate from a people's social and political culture. Smith suggested that to understand the basic foundations on which the primitive Semitic religions were based, one had to make a thorough study of the ritual (sacrificial) institutions. Since these tended to remain unchanged from the earliest times to the historical period, they reflected the fundamental beliefs that stood at the beginning of religious development. He subsequently found "a consistent unity of scheme," which ran through the whole historical development, from a crude and imperfect understanding of religious truth to a clear and full perception of its spiritual significance.

Working along the lines of Robertson Smith, Sir James G. Frazer published his famous work *The Golden Bough* (1890), which grew from two volumes in the first edition to twelve, twenty years later. This work studies the traditional rites and superstitious practices of primitive peoples and presents a great number of suppositions regarding the evolution of primitive religions. However, the vast accumulation of illustrative data is frequently more impressive than the conclusions drawn from them.

The faults of Frazer's methodology were those of nineteenth-century anthropologists in general, for they failed to understand that monotheistic religion could not be explained as developing out of primitive cults. While other theories were suggested by Wilhelm Wundt[33] and Johannes Pedersen,[34] these approaches failed to explain the transition from a primitive mentality to the highly developed conceptions of a later age, especially in the framework of the *Tanach* with its distinctive features and its religion.

In the meantime, another school had emerged: the Religio-Historical School of Interpretation. This field of research is known in German as *Religionsgeschichte*. The term "Comparative Religion," which is sometimes applied to it, connotes the early anthropological approach to religion and fails to indicate the importance of its historical aspect. Generally speaking, it is the application of the historical method to the study of religion, under the influence of positivist principles of investigation combined with the use of the comparative method. Auguste Comte made the point that one had to take the concrete and actual into consideration in philosophy; thus, this positive approach became influential in religious studies as well.[35]

No longer were broad generalizations about religion to be permitted. Rather, careful study of the historical manifestation of religion was researched. With the recovery of religious literature of the Far East, the publication of large numbers of inscriptions from the Graeco-Roman world, and the critical reexamination of the surviving documents of classical literature, the new approach acquired rich material with which to work.

The major point that this school propounded was that these discoveries showed that the ancient Orient represented a high cultural maturity—something denied by Wellhausen and others—and that Torah (and *Nach*) had been the outcome of this maturity. Some scholars rejected the evolutionary view of Israel's religious history and described the religion of *Tanach* as having already reached the full development of its most important features in the age of Moshe. Paul Volz argued that the high ethical principles of the Decalogue, which were usually attributed to prophetic inspiration, were

known to the Israelites in Moshe's time.[36] On the basis of the
evidence, Volz declared that the Mosaic authorship of the
Decalogue could easily be established and that it was as advanced as the later teachings of the Prophets. The most significant attempt to restore the traditional view of the Mosaic
religion was made by Bruno Baentsch, who claimed that traces
of monotheism can be found in other religions of the ancient
Orient.[37] Moreover, the discovery of the Hammurabi Code
in 1902—a code of ethics of a remarkably high standard—
completely changed the picture of the ancient Far East. Some
suggested that this code was the forerunner of the Torah law,
a view that was later rejected.[38] The difficulty of this approach
is that Hammurabi's monotheistic ideas do not seem to agree
with the monotheistic idea of the one Invisible God described
in the Old Testament. Also, the laws of the Torah often contradicted the Hammurabi Code.

As was the case with other schools, speculation became
more and more rife. It became clear that the Torah and the
other books of *Tanach* could best be understood on their own
merits, without extrabiblical evidence. Israel's religious history had characteristic features of its own that could not be
understood without primary attention being given to evidence derived from the Bible itself.

In his classic work *Critique of Religion and Philosophy*
(Princeton, NJ: Princeton University Press, 1978) p. 377,
Walter Kaufmann discusses Wellhausen's as well as other
forms of Higher Criticism and shows one of the major failures of these schools in the following observation:

Imagine a Higher Critic analyzing Goethe's Faust, which was
written by a single human being in the course of sixty years.
The scenes in which the heroine of Part One is called Gretchen
would be relegated to one author; the conflicting concep-

tions of the role of Mephistopheles would be taken to call for further divisions, and the Prologue in Heaven would be ascribed to a later editor, while the prelude on the stage would be referred to yet a different author. Our critic would have no doubt whatsoever that Part Two belongs to a different age and must be assigned to a great many writers with widely different ideas. The end of Act IV, for example, points to an anti-Catholic author who lampoons the church, while the end of Act V was written by a man, we should be told, who, though probably no orthodox Catholic, was deeply sympathetic to Catholicism. Where do we find more inconsistencies in style and thought and plan: in Goethe's Faust or in the Five Books of Moses?[39]

In short, inconsistencies of style and text cannot be taken as proof that a work was written by more than one author.

This is not the only observation Kaufmann makes concerning the nature of *Tanach*. After asking how *Tanach* should be read, he answers (p. 383):

Any suggestion of the close affinity of religion and poetry is generally met with the retort that a religious scripture is not mere poetry, which is true enough. But at the very least one might accord a religious scripture the same courtesy which one extends to poetry and recall Goethe's dictum: "What issues from a poetic mind wants to be received by a poetic mind. Any cold analyzing destroys the poetry and does not generate any reality. All that remains are potsheds which are good for nothing and only incommode us."

His observation is true in its critical attitude not only toward Higher Criticism but toward most of the other schools of Old Testament research as well. The different schools approached the Old Testament as a collection of historical facts from which to draw only such conclusions as the facts warranted.

It was the theological approach to Old Testament studies that, after long being neglected, made this point. The real
value of Torah and the other books of *Tanach* is essentially
religious in content and outlook and, as such, the critical
schools missed the point the Torah was making. Consequently, they used the wrong tools of investigation. Only an
approach to the world of Torah and *Nach* that did justice to
what it said about God, man, and the meaning of life could
offer a means of arriving at the permanent significance of the
Torah.

This point, for ages emphasized by traditional Jewish
scholars, had been made by Otto Eissfeldt[40] and later by
Walter Eihrodt,[41] albeit these studies were also heavily influenced by New Testament sentiments. Still these studies are
of major importance, for it took courage to present this view
at a time when the Torah and the rest of *Tanach* was rejected
as a "Jewish book" of no significance to Germans and Christians. It is only in the last twenty to thirty years, especially in
America and England, that full emphasis was given to this
approach. One of the most important books accepting the
true signifance of Torah and *Nach* was written by H. H.
Rowley and is entitled, *The Relevance of the Bible.*[42] Norman
H. Snaith's important work *The Distinctive Ideas of the Old
Testament* (London, 1944) also drew attention to the uniqueness of the Hebrew tradition.

In 1946, the secular German literary critic and theorist
Erich Auerbach published an essay called "Odysseus Scar."
In this important study he explored the nature of the biblical
narrative. In comparing it with the Homeric way of narrative, Auerbach shows how much the biblical narrative is different from the Greek epic. Unlike Homer, the former is
"fraught with background," unspoken words, and silence. It
can only be understood on its own terms. It is in need of

constant interpretation, claims absolute truth, and draws its reader into the world of religious experience. But above all, it is not art but *command* that strikes the student as the most important characteristic of the biblical story.

Auerbach maintained that the text of the Torah clearly shows that it wants to be "heard" as an encounter in which God speaks to man. It was not the later Rabbis or theologians who invented such a claim, but the very intent of the text itself.[43] Auerbach's essay gave impetus to much novel research in the field of Bible studies. Most important are the works of Robert Alter,[44] Roland Barthes,[45] and Harold Fisch.[46] All of them show a remarkable sensitivity for the authentic meaning of the text, reflecting a more "Jewish" approach when discussing some of the most difficult biblical narratives. Meir Weiss,[47] Meir Sternberg,[48] and Shimon bar Efrat,[49] using literary analysis, have dealt with the intricate subtleties of the biblical texts, uncovering more traditional interpretations. While these developments fall short in the eyes of traditional Judaism, they indicate a more objective, honest approach toward the Torah. The authors, dissociating themselves from the old schools of Bible Criticism, tried hard to hear the genuine "voice" of the Torah, and therefore moved closer to the traditional Jewish approach than any of their predecessors.

What has become increasingly clear is that the problems raised by Spinoza, Wellhausen, and others were well known to the traditional Jewish commentaries throughout the ages. What is different is the *method* by which these problems were solved. The Bible critics took it for granted that the biblical texts were texts like any other and therefore to be explored by the normal criteria of literary research. Axiomatically, without sincerely considering other possibilities, they rejected the idea of a "personal" God, the possibility of verbal revelation, and the authority of tradition in interpreting these texts.[50]

Mordechai Breuer, an Orthodox Jewish scholar, goes even as far as to state that he is prepared to accept much of the critic's findings. Using an unusual hybrid of neo-Kantian thought and Jewish mysticism, he concludes (not without major problems) that the traditional and the critical views are both "true." He distinguishes between the Torah as a "document" (phenomenon) and as words "written in black and white fire" (noumenon).[51] Thereupon, he asks why the word of God came down to man in such a way that it seems to support some of the critic's findings. He answers that this was necessary to show all the different religious perspectives of the Torah. For example, when discussing the different Pentateuchal names for God (one of the most important foundations of the Wellhausen theory for the existence of "documents"), he explains that this is connected with the different attributes of God as understood by the Jewish tradition. Sometimes God appears to us as a merciful God (the Tetragrammaton), at another time as Judge (*Elohim*). These, however, are the ways in which God *appears* to us (phenomenon). But behind all this is the mystical meaning of the Torah, which *unites* all these names (noumenon).[52]

The famous Rabbi Avraham Yitzchak Kook (1865-1935) added that there could essentially be no conflict between the scientific approach and the religious one. This was due to the fact that the Torah was primarily concerned with the knowledge of God and the sanctification of life, not with astronomy or geology. Scientific statements in the Torah and later prophets have to be understood as parables and analogies and not as primitive scientific statements.[53]

The greatest problem with Bible Criticism must, however, be seen in its failure to understand the crucial role the Oral Torah plays in the proper understanding of the Pentateuchal text. As stated before, the text can be understood only when read in its own spirit. Looking a little deeper, this means that it can be understood only when one "hears" its words in "the doing," in other words, when one "lives" it and is part of its weltanschauung. One can *read* the text of the "Pentateuch" and remain unaffected; in contrast, one can *listen* to the "Torah" as a religious act and be involved.[54]

More and more Bible scholars in the latter years admit that this is possible only when one studies the Pentateuchal text from *within* a certain tradition on which the text heavily relies. This is indeed one of the most important claims made by the Jewish tradition. Many Jewish commentators have convincingly argued that it is wholly *impossible* to understand the text without such a tradition. The point that they were making is that not only is it *possible* to read the text through the eyes of an Oral Tradition but that the intended meaning is the very one suggested by the Oral Tradition. While some modern commentaries may not go as far as arguing for a talmudic Oral Tradition, they do agree that the Pentateuchal text alludes to a comprehensive Oral Tradition that preceded it.[55]

In his famous commentary on the Torah, Rabbi Samson Raphael Hirsch argues that the Written Torah is the masterful "synopsis" of the Oral Tradition as laid down in the Talmud: first God instructed Moshe concerning the Oral Torah, and only afterward did He give him a dictation of the written text. In much the same way that lecture notes can help us to reproduce the original lecture only *after* we have heard it in full, so the Written Torah can only be understood after one has studied the Oral Torah in all its aspects: "It is not the Oral Law (Torah) which has to seek the guarantee of its authenticity in the Written Law (Torah); on the contrary, it is the Written Law (Law) which has to look for its warrant in the Oral Tradition."[56]

Yeshayahu Leibowitz, one of the most controversial Orthodox scholars of today, argues on similar lines: The sanctity and the uniqueness of the Written Torah cannot be inferred from any quality of the text itself.[57] Getting very close to the kabbalistic tradition, he states that *as* literature, the Written Torah is inferior to Shakespeare; *as* philosophy, it cannot compete with Plato or Kant, and *as* "moral education," Sophocles' *Antigone* is superior![58] Where the critics went wrong was to try to read and understand the "notes" without having heard the lecture. This would obviously perforce lead to the most absurd propositions. To read the Torah as an autonomous text is therefore an unforgivable mistake: "This kind of bibliolatry is Lutheran," says Leibowitz.

Important in a different way are the observations of Rabbi J. B. Soloveitchik, who deals with several "contradictions" in the Pentateuchal text. These, he shows, are not the result of having been written by a different hand but are rather evidence for different and paradoxical dimensions in the human condition with which the religious personality has to struggle.[59]

What can be said with certainty is that honest Bible scholars no longer maintain that the Torah is the result of different fragments edited and reedited. The Torah is now taken to be Mosaic in origin and content, and it has been acknowledged that much of this tradition was already well established in pre-Mosaic times. Although this position has moved considerably in the direction of the Jewish traditional view, it has definitely not thrown in the towel to the tradition concerning the verbal infallibility of the Torah.

A sister school of "Higher Criticism," known as "Lower Criticism," has come to the fore within the last centuries. This school has taken upon itself to question the reliability of the text based on outside sources such as the Septuagint. The proponents of this school have developed recensions based on variant readings that they regard as more reliable than the traditional text. As later scholars have pointed out, these recensions have been accomplished by offering baseless emendations and conjectures that are without rational foundation.

Nijberg has shown that these methods of critical analysis were in vogue in the latter part of the nineteenth century and were often employed in classical philology.[60] He mentions a scholar who used this approach to analyze *Paradise Lost* and came to the conclusion that this work was full of later interpolations. He also speaks of a scholar who made seven hundred revisions in Horace and finally published a volume that contained, in effect, a revised version of the poems which, while hardly being improved upon, turned out to be rather amusing.

Regarding "Lower Criticism," Nijberg observes:

> The most insane arbitrariness in this field is slowly beginning to recede. . . . The first step to such reflection, however, must be the recognition of the errors in method that have so far been made in the treatment of the text. . . . In the end we should remember a good old philological rule: When one does not understand something, one should first mistrust oneself and not the text.[61]

As has been clearly demonstrated, the Jewish Sages and later scribes were extraordinarily careful to guarantee that no changes were made in the text of the Torah and *Nach*.[62] Their precision was such that today, despite the fact that the Jews were dispersed to almost every corner of the globe and their communities often had little contact with each other, there are no essential differences in the text of the Torah scrolls. The Torah text that Jews brought from Cochin, India, is identical to the text used by the community in Cracow, Poland.

Still, there are differences in *some* ancient versions. This is not surprising: from the earliest times many individuals wrote scrolls for *private* study. These private scrolls often contained emendations that reflected the Oral Torah connected with a specific phrase or verse. This was done so as to remind oneself of the correct interpretation of the text. These scrolls were not intended for public use and were, in fact, ritually unfit for use because of these changes. Jewish tradition informs us that one of the great earlier Sages, Rabbi Meir, used to mark his allegorical explanations in his own private scroll as a means of remembering them.[63] There is no evidence of these private scrolls ever becoming mixed up with the traditional written Torah, for Jewish law is extremely precise and exacting in its demands of the scrolls used for the Torah reading in the synagogues. Scribes who prepared Torah scrolls were and are required to use a copy of the traditional Torah text as a source and are prohibited from writing a scroll from memory.

It is possible that non-Jewish editions of the Bible, such as the Septuagint or Vulgate, may have used private scrolls as a source, and this would account for the deviations found there.

But perhaps the most devastating blow to these critical theories was delivered by Rabbi Chaim Heller (1878-1960). Not only had he mastered the Oral Torah to the extent that he was one of the greatest talmudic scholars of his time, but he also knew every extant ancient Bible translation in its original target language, whether Aramaic, Greek, Latin, or Syriac. In his *Untersuchungen ueber die Peschitta* (1911), he took issue with those who concluded that apparent divergences from the Torah in their possession were due to variae lectiones in the ancient texts. Not so, he asserted. Every translation is a commentary, and the variations result from the translator preferring one explanation in the Oral Torah to another. Thus, the differences were exegetical rather than textual. He further showed that all the apparent differences stemmed from the thirty-two exegetical rules of biblical interpretation enumerated by Rabbi Elazar ben Rabbi Shimon.[64] In the above-mentioned study he gives examples showing how the translator employed each rule in his version.

Dr. David Hoffmann points out that even to accept the contention that the text in certain places of the Torah has been altered would still leave no choice but to accept the traditional version as the one closest to the original, for "every conjecture, no matter how many exegetical and historical and critical arguments it may be supported, does not offer us even the probability that the Prophet or the writer of Scripture wrote in this form and not in the text before us."[65]

On many occasions, seemingly "unintelligible" words of *Tanach* have suddenly become understandable in light of research and comparison with other oriental languages. It is due to this late research that the traditional text has grown in stature and respectability in the eyes of critical scientists and is increasingly preferred in many cases over other versions that were once considered accurate.

In summation, while Bible Criticism has found its way back to a more traditional approach, as far as the Pentateuchal text, its date, and its origin are concerned, one should never forget that the question of the *verbal infallibility* of the Torah as the expression of an explicit divine revelation lies outside the scope of any literal or scientific investigation.

The modern crisis of religion, of which Bible Criticism is a symptom, is due to the misapplication of scientific research to aspects of reality, like faith and revelation, to which they do not belong. Laws deduced from the world of nature cannot explain supernatural phenomena, in the same way that no scientist would ever accept the position that the rules governing why organic materials react to certain stimuli could apply to inorganic substances. Both are intrinsically different in nature and can only be understood as two completely different systems.

The Torah is a covenantal document and is to be studied as such. It does not inform us of "facts," "history," or "anthropology." It reveals a continuous encounter between God and man, which was set in motion with the revelation at Sinai. It cannot be read but only studied, proclaimed, heard, and experienced. The encounter with its text is a religious act and therefore prefaced with a blessing. For this reason it is untouched and unimpaired by the results of Bible Criticism.

What is important to realize is that the struggle over the origin of the text of the Torah was, and is, not just an academic one. It is foremost a battle between "divine authority" and "human autonomy." Modernity, starting with Spinoza, was looking for ways through which it could liberate itself from the biblical worldview and its far-reaching divine demands. Since it was this biblical text that made man submissive to divine authority, it was necessary to start an assault on the biblical text itself and strip it of its divine nature. The interplay between sociology and theology is a complex one, but what is clear is that *what* man will find and conclude is greatly dependent on the question of *why* he is looking. The Torah can be made to yield whatever meaning its interpreters like to assign to it.

This fact is also of great importance in understanding what has happened within the Jewish community over the last two hundred years. In an attempt to become part of the secular world, many Jews looked to Bible Criticism as a most forceful (and welcome) source of legitimization for the break with tradition. In reference to what Heinrich Heine once called "the portable fatherland of the Jew," the Torah was historicized, secularized, and fragmentized. It is hardly possible to ignore the fact that since the day when this fragmentation theory made inroads into the Jewish community, the Jewish People has lost much of its élan vital. It resulted in "nontraditional" forms of Judaism and eventually caused Jews to turn their backs on tradition altogether. The secularization of the Torah had led to secularization of the people.

11

On Speech and Prayer

ewish prayer is not an easy matter.[1] It requires, on the one hand, great concentration and much devotion, and on the other, the careful recitation of words that were written by human beings who lived nearly two thousand years ago. On the one hand, there is an inner need for isolation and solitude when speaking to God. On the other, there is the obligation to pray in the presence of the community (*minyan*—ten men). There is tension between these different requirements.

Kavanah, concentration, also means inwardness and devotion. It is the free outpouring of the human heart to the heavenly Father. It is an experience of great trembling, of ultimate aspirations—a fire in the soul. Nothing can describe this experience. It is touching heaven through human words. Such prayer is not bound by a certain number of words, as Moshe interceding for the People Israel after the incident with the Golden Calf, prays for forty days a prayer of intense devotion before he is answered (Deuteronomy 9:18).

At another time, only five of his precious words heal his

sister Miriam from a dangerous disease: "O Lord, heal her, I beseech You" (Numbers 12:13).

No doubt, Moshe did not use a prayer book when he spoke all these words. In fact, such a possibility would strike us as offensive. The grandeur of these prayers lies in their wondrous nature of spontaneity. The Talmud even suggests that the use of prayer books is to be compared to the burning of a scroll of the Torah![2] Indeed, from all the ancient sources it is clear that biblical man was used to praying in a spontaneous way and was probably opposed to the very idea of using a prayer book when standing before his Lord.

Also, most organized *daily* prayer sessions as readers know them today do not seem to have existed in the ancient world. Many, like some people today, felt the need for isolation at the hour of prayer. A *minyan* did not stand as central to the world of Jewish prayer as it stands today.

King David's ebullient words stating that "the mountains are skipping like rams, and the hills like lambs before the Lord" were not written on a word processor or under the pressure of an editor's deadline. Nor were they said in the presence of a *minyan*!

What, then, is the reason Jewish tradition today requires a *minyan* and a prayer book, both obstacles to a really deep, devotional, and spontaneous prayer?

CHUTZPAH

Prayer is a *chutzpah* (impertinence). How does man dare to speak to God, the Master of the Universe? The presumption that man can just open his mouth and God will listen is simply unheard of! When trying to get an audience with the queen, much paperwork has to be done, many committee meetings with ministers and officials have to be set up, and security checks and other conditions have to be fulfilled. Only then—and not always—may one see the queen for a few minutes! But speaking with the Lord of all lords, the King of all kings, man has the impertinence to believe that no previous audiences are required, no security checks needed.

More than that, one does not even have to come to the royal palace; one can stay at home; find oneself on an army base, shop, or bank; be dressed in pajamas or flying on an airplane. Not even a knock at the door is required to come and have an audience! The implications of this defy all imagination.

Aristotle, probably in reference to Plato, once remarked, "Everybody may criticize him, but who is permitted to praise him?" Goethe, the great German poet, expressed himself in a similar way: "Wer einen lobt, stellt sich ihm gleich" (He who praises another person places himself on the other's level). What right does man have to praise God?

And still, mortal, limited man can address himself to the Lord of Eternity! This is what bothered the Sages of Israel: How will man ever dare to pray? How will Judaism motivate men to participate in an impertinence of incredible proportions without running the risk of becoming haughty—to make man audacious and still ask him to be humble!

THE FIRST *CHUTZPAH*-NIKS

Who were the first ones to dare to speak to God? Who were the first *chutzpah*-niks who instigated man's dialogue with the Master of the Universe? No doubt, they were biblical figures such as Adam, Chavah, Avraham, Yitzchak, and Ya'akov. They dared to open their mouths. Their unprec-

edented humility became the very foundation through
which they could speak. They felt God in all their bones,
in their very existence. Modern man, however, cannot stand
on his own two feet. His haughtiness and lack of religious sense force him to hide behind these great biblical
figures.

Imagine if modern man had been the first to speak to
God! Who would have dared? It would have been unbear-
able and a great embarrassment, even a scandal. No man in
his right mind would have thought of such an impertinence!

Our justification for praying is, however, clear: we are
not the instigators! We just continue a conversation of more
than five thousand years, started by men and women who
really dared and knew the art of prayer! We are in good
company; we just build on a long-established contact. This
is, no doubt, the reason we start our most important prayer,
the *Shemoneh Esreh* (the eighteen benedictions), with the
words, "God of Avraham, God of Yitzchak, God of Ya'akov."
We can stand before God only when we remind ourselves
that we continue this daring conversation only because others started it. *We did not start it!*

In other words we do not stand alone before God—we
stand in the company of five thousand years of continuous
prayer! But "standing together" does not only mean to stand
in the company of all our ancestors; it also means to stand
together with our fellowmen "today." While prayer in solitude has many advantages (of which, at times, one should
make use), community prayer offers the possibility to dare
to open our mouths. In the company of the community,
strengthened by our feeling of brotherhood, we dare to speak
words to God that we would not say on our own! This is
one of the great advantages of *minyan* prayers over prayers
in solitude.

WHICH WORDS?

It is one thing to dare to pray, but quite another to know *what* to say. When a delegation is invited to speak to the queen to impress upon her the importance of certain community matters, many hours of preparation and careful deliberation precede the actual meeting. Every word will be carefully considered. Many discussions will take place to make sure that things are said in a clear, concise way with no superfluous words. Every word counts! Every sentence is vital!

How much more true this is when speaking to the Lord of the Universe! To say the *right* words to the King of kings is an act of great profundity. Not everybody knows this art. Only those who are well versed in the art of idiom and phraseology will find the right words. Only those who know the inner chambers of the human heart will know the skill to bring the right "nusach" (word use) of a prayer into being.

Moreover, not everything that comes from the mouth of man should come to the ear of God! Which requests are noble and worthy? Which are humiliating and undeserving?

MODERN MAN AND LAUDATIONS

While biblical man still knew the answer to these questions, modern man is too self-conscious to know what is worthy and what is not. He needs to know that he is asking in accordance with the great foundations of his religion—requests and even praises that are sanctified by his tradition. When praying in accordance with the prayer book, the Jew is confident that he is asking for that which is religiously and ethically worthwhile and correct and acceptable to God.

Moreover, which praises are worthy laudations? When is one really praising God, and when does one think that one is praising God while in fact doing Him a great disservice? Once Rabbi Chanina observed a man praising God with many different epithets: "great," "mighty," "powerful," "majestic," "awesome," "strong," "fearless," "sure," "honored," and so forth. After this "deeply religious" man had finished, the Sage asked him "if that was all." When you start praising God, you can never stop. Man can begin praising God but never end. Therefore, it is better to be humble, to say only a few distinct words of praise as formulated by our forefathers and printed in our prayer book and then revert back to silent humility. "It is as if an earthly king had a million denari of gold, and someone praised him as possessing silver ones. Would it not be an insult to him?"[3]

Fixed prayers enlarge the range of that which should be man's concern. Not only are all communal prayers formulated in the plural ("Give us"), but they also are prayers for the welfare of the community.

In a well-known passage in the Jerusalem Talmud we are told that the Kohen Gadol, the high priest, used to say a most disturbing prayer on Yom Kippur (Day of Atonement).[4] On this most Holy Day of the Jewish year, in which the high priest asks for spiritual and material blessings, he also prays that God should "not listen to the prayers of the wayfarers"— to the requests of one substantial section of the population! One wonders how such a prayer could be said on any day of the year, let alone on Yom Kippur! What was it about the prayers of the wayfarers that required the high priest on Yom Kippur to ask God not to listen to them? Moreover, does God not know which prayers to accept and which to reject? Does He need the advice of the high priest?

The wayfarers, however, did a most unfortunate thing. They asked God to withhold rain although the nation was in great need of it! They asked God to protect them from the rain when they found themselves on the road. Such a prayer is egocentric. It runs against the needs of the nation. Rain is crucial to the Land of Israel to this very day! Israel's economy depends on it. The high priest prayed for this timely rain, one of the greatest concerns of the nation. Israel is lost without rain! The wayfarers, however, had "more important" things on their minds—a dry journey! Preoccupied by their own inconveniences, they totally ignored the needs of the nation at large. When the *Kohen Gadol* asks God to ignore these prayers, he is not advising God which prayers to accept and which to reject, he is teaching the nation of Israel that prayers are only worthy when they are uttered for the benefit of the whole community, even in the face of one's personal needs! Fixed prayers are, therefore, prayers that prevent man from falling into the trap of selfishness.

FINDING THE RIGHT WORDS

When modern man needs to pray and to pour out his heart before his Maker, he may find himself in a most awkward position. He will have great difficulty in finding the right words to express his innermost feelings. Modern man lacks the vocabulary to say what is on his heart. This is even more true of man in recent decades. His heart cannot land on the shore of his lips. But when man opens his prayer book looking for words he does not know, he makes a most surprising discovery: "*These are exactly the words I was looking for but that I could not find!"* This is the great advantage of fixed prayers.

The Sages of Israel, in carefully analyzing the human heart with all its complexities and frustrations, found, after much contemplation and deliberation, the words that would carry the inner needs of man's heart to his lips.

THE MUSIC OF PRAYER

One may object that this is altogether impossible. How could it ever be that all men could express their inner feelings with exactly the same words as the standard prayer book seems to suggest?

This is, however, far from what is suggested. A prayer book is like a composition of musical notes of a famous symphony. When a musician plays a Mozart violin concerto, he does not *play* the notes; rather, he *borrows* Mozart's musical notes. A great, talented musician is somebody who plays the music of his own heart, but he externalizes them onto the notes of the master composer. The vibrations, the movement of the fingers with their particular unique "touch," express the deeper emotions of the gifted violinist. The music notes, however, are fixed, not to be changed. This is the power of the real prayer book—notes holding the potential music of everybody's heart. The praying man plays his inner prelude on the musical notes of Israel's great composers, its Sages. Musicians involved in their orchestral score not only lift their audiences to heavenly spheres, they inspire each other to discover new dimensions of their own souls as well. Similarly, the participants in the community prayer play the serenades of their souls which provoke, through a moment of artistic symbiosis, previously unknown worlds in the hearts of their fellow *minyan* participants.

The fixed prayers hold still another advantage: they connect many generations of Jews throughout their long history. The Jewish community would not be the same if today's prayer was something totally different from yesterday's. Neither would its members share similar feelings and emotions. And since the Jew should not pray in the isolation of his own little world, but as a member of his people, as a *shaliach* (messenger) of his nation, community prayer becomes vital.

When finding himself in Jerusalem, New York, or Tokyo, a Jew will immediately feel at home when stepping into a synagogue. Nothing is strange to him. Instead he finds the same prayers, the same customs, the feeling of familiarity. It is like a homecoming in strange surroundings. He does not feel alone but turns to a four-thousand-year-old world where all his parents and grandparents lived.

Fixed prayers are also dreams. They tell the Jewish People where their priorities should lie and what they should be dreaming of. When a Jew is told to pray for the return of the Temple service and its sacrifices, he may not be capable of saying these petitions with the greatest amount of devotion. He may even feel totally detached, and possibly disturbed, by such prayers. The Sages, by making man say these and similar prayers, express an important message—the Temple service is crucial for your personal relationship with God and is of great value to the entire Jewish People. As long as the Temple has not been rebuilt, we Jews are not ourselves. How, then, is it that you are not dreaming of the day when the Sanctuary will again stand in Jerusalem? Your heart has not yet grasped the im-

portance of the Temple service, so there is still a long way
to go!

Every morning, afternoon, and evening, the prayer book
takes the worshiper on a journey to the great visions of pos-
terity and makes him partake of a world that the faculties of
his appreciation may not yet have reached.

MOOD

What if one is not in the mood to pray? What if the inner
music of the soul is in confinement and cannot break
through? Should one just forget about it until one suddenly
becomes inspired, when one's mood is once more in the right
spirit?

What does the musician do when he is not in the mood
for playing music? Does he stop practicing? The musician
knows one thing—to stop practicing is suicidal. The lack of
practice will make any later attempt only harder, if not impossible. It will most probably be the end of his career. To
continue to play and practice is vital. Moreover, one gets into
the mood for playing music only by playing music! To wait
for the moment when this mood will return is a futile undertaking.

By continuing to play, one keeps alive the ability to play!
So, too, with the praying man: his ability to pray will stay
alive only by praying at times when his soul is cold and his
heart empty. And could it perhaps be true that just at the
time when one's soul is cold and praying is hard, one's prayer
is most sincere? A prayer said in the painful knowledge of
one's own inability to connect with God may quite well be
the most exalted form of divine service.

SILENT PRAYER

Why must some prayers be said aloud and others in silence? Why is the most important prayer, the *Shemoneh Esreh* (eighteen benedictions) in the Jewish prayer book, to be said in a whisper? There is something most profound about this. When the Jew rises early in the morning to go and speak to His Maker, his soul is still cold. He needs to be warmed up, so as "to get into it." When he enters the synagogue, he will try to get his spiritual engine running. It needs to be woken up—it needs to "be turned on" before it will run smoothly and at full power. The early-morning blessings are like the turning of the key that warms up the engine. After the first stirrings, the second "gear" is set in motion. This is done through the *Pesukei De-Zimra*, the great Songs of King David. Slowly, the whole personality of man becomes involved; his body becomes part of his soul and starts to play on the spiritual music notes of the prayer. Slowly, it becomes time to accelerate into a higher gear: *Kabbalat Malchut Shamayim*, the acceptance of the kingdom of heaven. A transformation of the human personality is taking place. Man is entering into the chambers of the King Himself. His voice gets louder, his emotions more intensified. He can no longer hold himself back. The proximity of the King makes him cry out, "Hear O Israel, the Lord Our God, the Lord Is One!" By this time his prayer has reached its peak. Now, standing in front of the King, he will have to plead for his life, his food, his health.

Suddenly, a paradox takes form. On the one hand, he needs to shout, like somebody standing on top of a huge tower, any moment falling to his death, asking for help and mercy; on the other hand, standing in front of the King renders him totally speechless, like a child not having seen his father for years, running into his arms and shouting "Abba, Abba." Like a child running to his father and falling into his arms, no longer capable of uttering a word, so does the Jew fall into the arms of his Maker—and words can no longer express his emotions. Silence prevails. The connection is too deep, too overpowering. Still, that very silence holds the words for deeply emotional prayer: "Please do not leave me, but sustain me." So does the Jew reenact this great emotional moment and is consequently told to be silent, to remind him that if he understands the implications of his "run" to his Father, he should no longer be able to speak—total silence. So why does the *halachah* tell him to continue to pray, but only in a whisper? To teach him that while he may not yet have acquired such a feeling of total ecstasy, he should *partially* act as if he has, so as to teach him how far he still has to go—that is the *Shemoneh Esreh*.

Notes

CHAPTER 1

1. *Guide for the Perplexed* 3:32.
2. Laws of the Kings 11:1.
3. The *Shemoneh Esreh* prayer, Section: *Retzeh* (the eighteen-benediction prayer that is said every morning, afternoon, and evening).
4. *Guide for the Perplexed* 3:32.
5. On Exodus 25:9.
6. Ibid.
7. T. B. *Berachot* 33b.
8. See his observation in the *Guide for the Perplexed* 3:46.
9. T. B. *Sukkah* 41a. This could be inferred from Rashi.
10. *Nefesh Ha-Chaim* 3:11.

CHAPTER 2

1. *Genesis Rabbah* 11.
2. See Maimonides, *Guide for the Perplexed* 1:1;*Yesodei Ha-Torah* 4:8.
3. See Rabbi J. B. Soloveitchik, "The Lonely Man of Faith," *Tradition* 7:2 (Summer 1965): 11-12.

4. *Genesis Rabbah* 11.

5. Rabbi Levi Ben Gershom, *Commentary on Bereshit* (Edition Bomberg), p. 15.

6. See Nechama Leibowitz, *Studies in Shemot* (Jerusalem: World Zionest Organization, Department for Torah Education and Culture, 1972), pp. 696-699.

7. See Eliyahu Kitov, *The Book of Our Heritage*, vol. 3 (Jerusalem: Feldheim, 1978), p. 76.

8. Mishnah, *Shabbat* 7:2.

9. T. B. *Shabbat* 49a.

10. Dayan Dr. I. Grunfeld, *The Sabbath, A Guide to Its Understanding and Observance* (New York: Feldheim, 1959), p. 15.

11. Rashi, loc. cit.

12. Albert Schweitzer, speech at the occasion of his acceptance of the Nobel Peace Prize, quoted in Erich Fromm, *To Have or To Be?* (New York: HarperCollins, 1976), p. 12.

13. Ibid., pp. 57-58.

14. *Havdalah:* A ceremony that asks the Jew to take a lighted torch, spices, and wine, after which he declares the end of the Sabbath.

CHAPTER 3

1. C. G. Jung, *Essays on Contemporary Events* (1936; repr., London: Kegan Paul, 1947), chap. 1, "Wotan."

2. Arnold Toynbee, *Study of History*, vol. 4 (1961), p. 262.

3. Quoted by S. Spiegel, *Hebrew Reborn* (1930), pp. 375-389.

4. *Sabbath Prayer Book of the Jewish Reconstructionist Foundation* (1954), p. xxi.

5. *Genesis Rabbah* 1:10.

6. T. B. *Sanhedrin* 38a.

7. Ibid., 59a.

8. See Rabbi Yechiel Jacov Weinberg, Responsa *Sridei Eish*, vol. 2 (Jerusalem: Mosad HaRav Kook, 1966), p. 104.

9. While there are no obligations to apply these moral directives in one's relationship with non-Jews, one is definitely permitted, and even encouraged, to do so. See, for example, Maimonides, *Laws of Robbery and Lost Property* 11:3 and *Beer Hagolah, Choshen Mishpat* 348:4.

10. Immanuel Kant, *Groundwork of the Metaphysics of Morals*, trans. H. J. Paton (London: Hutchinson, 1958) pp. 98-100.

11. Leopold Zunz, "Leiden," chap. 2 in *Synagogale Poesie des Mittelalters* (1836).

12. Nicholas Berdyaev, *The Meaning of History* (1963), pp. 86-87.

13. Mark Twain, quoted in *The Man That Corrupted Hadleyburg* (London: Chatto and Windus, 1898).

14. A. Leroy Beaulieu, *Israel among the Nations* (1893), quoted in Chief Rabbi J. H. Hertz, *A Book of Jewish Thoughts* (repr., Oxford University Press, 1966), p. 174.

15. Carl Mayer, "Religious and Political Aspects of Anti-Judaism." In *Jews in a Gentile World*, ed. Graebner and Britt (New York: Macmillan, 1942), p. 316.

16. Commentary on Genesis 10:9.

17. On Genesis 10:9.

18. S. R. Hirsch, Commentary on Genesis 11:1.

19. *Genesis Rabbah* 38:6.

20. Rabbi Simcha Zissel meKelm, *Chochmah U-Mussar*, vol. 2, p. 185.

21. *Pirke DeRabbi Eliezer* 24.

22. The difference between grand buildings and skyscrapers in fascist and "free" countries is that the citizens of the "free" countries are permitted to climb those buildings and have a view from above, while the fascist state will make sure that these buildings are not ascended. One is only allowed to look *up* to these buildings, never to look *down* from them.

23. *Genesis Rabbah* 38:7.

24. Erich Fromm, in his famous work *To Have or To Be?* (New York: HarperCollins, 1976), reminds the reader of the fact

that there is, for example, no Hebrew word for "to have." One can only say, "There is to me." ("*Yesh li.*") The sexual act in the Bible is an act of knowledge, not of possessing another person: "And Adam knew Eve" (Genesis 4:1).

25. Hirsch, Commentary on Genesis 11:7.

26. *Genesis Rabbah* 64:4.

27. *Genesis Rabbah* 1:42.

28. Ibid. 1:34.

29. On Genesis 12:5.

30. Obadiah Sforno on Exodus 19:5-6.

31. See chapter 5, "Particularism and Universalism."

32. It should be stated that since the establishment of the first Jewish Commonwealth, there has always been a percentage of Jews living outside the Land of Israel. Many of them were *shelichim* (messengers) who were sent by the people of Israel to establish cultural, political, and financial liaisons with the world community.

33. See, for example, Isaac Deutcher, *The Non-Jewish Jew and Other Essays* (New York: Oxford University Press, 1968).

34. This may explain why non-Jews who converted to Judaism are not yet part of *Kehal Ha-Shem*," "the congregation of the Lord," the mysterious collective experience of the Jewish People. See, for example, *Shulchan Aruch, Even Ha-Ezer* 4:22. On the other hand, they are considered full-fledged Jews, because they went through a similar "religious experience" as Avraham did, which, although lacking in the historical "root experience," must have been so overwhelming that it somehow resulted in a similar condition.

35. This is the "official" number of commandments in the Torah as given by T. B. *Makkot* 23b.

36. Tolstoy, quoted in J. H. Hertz, *A Book of Jewish Thoughts* (London: Oxford University Press, 1966).

37. T. B. *Sanhedrin* 56a. In general it must be said that non-Jews are permitted to keep any of the other commandments given to the People Israel. See *Shulchan Aruch, Orach Haim, Hilchot Shabbat*, 304; *Mishnah Berurah, Biur Halachah*, 25.

38. See the work of the great gentile Hebraist Hugo Grotius, *De Juri Belli ad Pacis*, seventeenth century. (For the radical character of Grotius's theory, see E. Bloch, *Naturrecht und menschliche wuerde* [Frankfurt am Main, 1961], pp. 63-64) and John Selden (*De Jure Naturale et gentium Juxta Disciplinam Ebraerum*, 1665), fathers of international law. For an informative study of this subject, see David Novak, *The Image of the Non-Jew in Judaism* (Lewiston, NY: Edwin Mellen Press, 1984) and Robert Gordis, *Judaic Ethics for a Lawless World* (New York: Jewish Theological Seminary of America, 1986).

39. T. B. *Bava Metzia* 59b.

40. See chapter 5, "On Particularism and Universalism."

CHAPTER 4

1. T. B. *Yevamot* 45b; *Shulchan Aruch, Even Ha-Ezer* 4:22.

2. *Karet*: Extirpation, a punishment at the hands of heaven. The *halachah* explains *karet* as premature death (50). (See *Sifra, Emor*, 14, 4; see also T. B. *Mo'ed Katan* 28a; T. J. *Bikkurim* 2:1, 64b).

3. *Kiddushin* 3:12; *Yevamot* 45b; *Shulchan Aruch, Even Ha-Ezer* 4:13.

4. T. B. *Sanhedrin* 69a-71a.

5. *Midrash Rabbah* On Ecclesiastes 4:1.

6. The Supreme High Court of ancient Israel.

7. John Hick, *Philosophy of Religion* (Englewood Cliffs, NJ: Prentice-Hall, 1983), p. 47.

8. T. B. *Gittin* 59b.

9. T. B. *Kiddushin* 72b.

CHAPTER 5

1. See also chapter 3, "On Jewish Identity and the Chosen People."

2. Israel is "only the first fruit of his increase" (Jeremiah 2:3). This, however, does not mean that Israel will eventually cease to exist. It will continue to exist, but with higher "purpose." See Isaiah 66:21 and *Tana De-Vei Eliyahu Zuta* 20. See also *Exodus Rabbah* 19:4.

3. Israel's genius is, however, received from God; see *Zohar* II 88b, 207a; III, 238b; *Zohar Chadash, Bereishit* 22; *Tikkunei Ha-Zohar* 6, 24, 48; *Kedushat Levi*, p. 2a.

4. *Mishneh Torah*, Laws of Idolatry I:3. See also Rabbi Samson Raphael Hirsch, *Nineteen Letters* (letter 9).

5. Quoted by J. H. Hertz, *A Book of Jewish Thoughts* (London: Oxford University Press, 1966), p. 131.

6. See Amos 3:2. Also see T. B. *Shabbat* 88a, T. B. *Avodah Zarah* 2b; T. B. *Chullin* 89a.

7. The Jewish Israel Zangwill (1864-1926). Zangwill once said, "If there were no Jews, they would have to be invented, for the use of politicians: they are indispensable, the antithesis of a panacea guaranteed to cause all evils" (*Speeches, Articles, and Letters* [London, 1937]).

One wonders if it is also true that if there were no State of Israel, it would have to be invented for the use of the politicians. . . .

8. *Pensees*, vol. 8.

9. See *Responsa Sridei Eish* 2:104. See p. 208; 3:8.

10. It is perhaps important to become aware of still another characteristic of the People Israel.

Even when Israel transgresses its mission as the Chosen People, it does *not* lose its "Chosen Identity." Israel lived through "root experiences." It encountered a constant flow of sufferings, trials, divine intervention, and miracles. This shaped the Jewish personality throughout the ages and fashioned it into a nation carrying all the "components" to become a "world-transforming people." Even the most assimilated Jew carries these components, built over four thousand years, in his very personality. This is the reason that Jewish law still sees him as a Jew: the Jew personifies these root experiences. He is the very result of these experiences.

The "replacement" theology does not seem to be aware of this important fact. See page 70.

11. *Sanhedrin* 38a.

12. *Tana De-Vei Eliyahu* 9.

13. *Berachot* 16a.

14. *Sanhedrin* 59a; see also *Sifra* on Leviticus 18:5.

15. *Kiddushin* 31a.

16. See Numbers, chap. 19.

17. Palestinian Talmud, *Bava Metzia* 34a.

18. *Gittin* 61a. See also Palestinian Talmud, *Gittin* 5:9.

19. *Genesis Rabbah* I.

20. *Sanhedrin* 56a-60a. See also *Mishneh Torah*, Laws of the Kings 8:10; 10:12; *Tosefta, Avodah Zarah* 8:4. For a full explanation see Nathan T. Lopes Cardozo, *The Infinite Chain* (New York: Targum Press, 1989), chaps. 1, 2.

21. *Sifri*, loc. cit.

22. *Malbim* on *Sifri*.

23. *Bava Kamma* 37b.

24. *Kol Sifrei Maharitz Chayot*, I (Jerusalem, 5718), p. 490.

25. *Ger toshav* (resident alien): A non-Jew who has been granted residence rights in the Jewish State by declaring he will abide by the seven commandments (Laws of Kings 8:10).

26. Yehudah Halevi's famous work on Jewish philosophy, *The Book of Argument and Proof in Defense of the Despised Faith* (10th-11th century).

27. See Maimonides, *Mishneh Torah*, Laws of the Kings 8:11.

28. See Rashi on Genesis 1:1.

CHAPTER 6

1. This essay was written before the momentous Israeli-Palestinian Agreement of September 1993.

2. *Genesis Rabbah* 61:4.

3. Rashi on Genesis 21:9.

4. *Genesis Rabbah* on Genesis 24:62.

5. Genesis 16:2, ad loc.

6. Ramban on Genesis 16:5.

7. Hirsch on Genesis 16:5. Samson Raphael Hirsch, *The Pentateuch, Translated and Explained*, trans. Isaac Levy (New York: Judaica Press, 1971).

8. Ibid., Genesis 16:14.

9. *Genesis Rabbah* 61.

10. Ad loc.

11. Rabbi Menachem Recanati, *Bereshit*, p. 8a; Va-Yetzei, pp. 28a, 29a.

CHAPTER 7

1. In a Torah scroll, most of the letters are written without crowns, for example, ה, and some are written with crowns, for example, ט.

2. *Pirke Avot* 5:22.

3. Menachem Recanati, *Ta'amei Ha-Mitzvot* (Basel, 1581), p. 3a. See also *Zohar* II, p. 60a.

4. *Genesis Rabbah* 1:1

5. Jerusalem Talmud, *Shekalim* 6:1, end.

6. *Sefer Yetzirah*, chap. 2. There are several variant texts of this classic kabbalistic work. All of them are included in the edition that was republished by Rabbi Mordechai Attiya (Jerusalem, 1972).

7. Rabbi Shlomo Eliashov, *Sefer Le-Shem She-Vo Ve-Achlama*, in the volume subtitled *Sefer Ha-Birurim* (Commentary on *Sefer Etz Chaim* of Rabbi Isaac Luria) (Jerusalem, 1973); sha'ar "Seder Atzilut," p. 2b.

8. *Zohar* III, p. 36a.

9. Ramban, *Introduction to Commentary on the Torah,* ed. by Dr. Chaim Dov Chavel (Jerusalem: Mosad HaRav Kook, 1973), pp. 6-7.

10. Rabbi Joseph Ibn Gikatila, *Sha'arei Orah* (Offenbach, 1715), introduction to first section, p. 2b.

11. The word *otam* can be written in the full form, with *vav*, or in the "short" form, without *vav*.

12. Ramban, *Introduction to Commentary on the Torah*.

13. See chapter 10, especially pp. 186-188.

14. T. B. *Shabbat* 88b.

15. *Mishneh Torah Yesodei Ha-Torah* 9:1.

16. Ibid.

17. *Midrash HaGadol* on Genesis 2:15.

18. Rabbi Avraham Azulai, *Chesed Le-Avraham* (Sulzbach, 1685), 2:11.

19. Ibid. 2:27.

20. Rabbi Chaim Vital, *Sha'ar Ma'amrei Razal* (1890), in back of the edition including *Sha'ar Ma'amrei Rashbi*, 16c.

21. Rabbi Isaac the Blind, commentary on *Midrash Konen* (in *Beit Midrash,* vol. 2, ed. Jellineck [1853] pp. 23-24). See also *Sefer HaBahir*, sec. 99.

22. T. B. *Menachot* 29b.

23. Rambam, *Shemonah Perakim*, chap. 7.

24. *Seder Yetzirat Ha-Vlad* (in *Bet Midrash*, a compilation of *midrashim*).

25. T. B. *Niddah* 30b.

26. Ibid.; *Berachot* 17a.

27. T. B. *Berachot* 6a, 7a.

28. *Pirke Avot* 6:2.

CHAPTER 8

1. Rudolf Otto, *The Idea of the Holy* (London, 1923; rev. ed. 1929).

2. London, 1930; quoted by E. F. Schumacher, *A Guide for the Perplexed* (New York: Harper Colophon Books, 1978), p. 42.

3. *Living Time* (London, 1952), chap. 1. Quoted in Schumacher, *A Guide for the Perplexed*, p. 33.

4. Ibid.

5. Ibid., p. 32.

6. Avraham Yehoshua Heschel, *Man's Quest for God, Studies in Prayer and Symbolism* (New York: Charles Scribner's Sons, 1954), p. xiii.

7. William James, *Principles of Psychology*, vol. 1 (New York: Macmillan and Co.).

CHAPTER 9

1. T. B. *Chullin* 115b. *Shulchan Aruch, Yoreh De'ah* 87:1; *Pitchei Teshuvah* 2.

2. T. B. *Pesachim* 29a; Exodus 12:19; 13:7.

3. One may wonder why God wished to create a world that would, after all, revert back to spirtuality. If God wished only spirtuality to prevail, why did He create a physical universe in the first place? The kabbalists respond by saying that the division between the spiritual and physical, originating with the creation act, allowed for the capacity of "longing," the urge and drive to bring unity to that which has been divided. This, they believe, is the greatest good that God wanted to bestow. Love, the most important substance in giving man the most exalted form of joy, is, after all, the result of two components *longing* to become one.

CHAPTER 10

1. This essay was written many years ago. Since then, I have updated it several times. To my pleasant surprise, I have found some similarities between this essay and some of the observations made by Chief Rabbi Dr. Jonathan Sacks from Great Britain. I have incorporated some of his insights from his book *Crisis and Covenant* (New York: Manchester University Press, 1992).

2. T. B. *Sanhedrin* 89a.

3. Maimonides, *Commentary to Mishnah: Introduction to Sanhedrin*, chap. 10, principle 8.

4. See Rabbi Chaim Hirschensohn's interesting discussion, *Malki Ba-Kodesh*, pt. 2. (St. Louis, MO: Moinester Printing Co., 1921), pp. 215-250, concerning the question of whether it is only the divinity of the Torah that is vital to Judaism or Moshe's "authorship" as well.

5. Benedictus de Spinoza, *A Theologic-Political Treatise* (New York: Dover, 1951), p. 165. Spinoza's conclusion was "that the word of God is faulty, mutilated, tampered with, and inconsistent, that we possess it only in fragments and that the original of the covenant which God made with the Jews has been lost." This observation is, for two reasons, most remarkable: First of all, Spinoza leaves the door open for a possible revelational experience. God *may* have spoken to the Jews, but the original text of that conversation was lost. This seems to conflict with Spinoza's understanding of a God who lacks all "personality" and henceforth is incapable of *ever* conversing with man. Second, it lays the foundation for what later became the attitude of Reform Judaism's understanding of the Pentateuchal text, which sees the text as some kind of human record of the Jews' encounter with God, and as such, "inspired." This idea contradicts Spinoza's general attitude, which sees the text as "primitive literature."

There are even earlier observations of this kind. One famous "Bible critic" was Chivi Al Balkhi (ninth century) of Persia. See "Geniza Specimens—The Oldest Collection of Bible Difficulties by a Jew," Solomon Schechter, *Jewish Quarterly Review* (old series) 13 (190): 345-374.

In Numbers, (chap. 16) we read of Korach, the first critic of Moses' authority, who claimed that "the Torah was not from heaven" (Jerusalem Talmud, *Sanhedrin* 10, *halachah* 1). Another earlier critic was Menashe the son of Hizkiah (698-543 B.C.E) "who examined biblical narratives to prove them worthless." Thus, he jeered: had Moses not anything else to write besides, "and Lothan's sister was Timnah"? (Genesis 36:12) (T. B. *Sanhedrin* 99).

6. Karl Heinrich Graf (1815-1869), a German Protestant Bible scholar on whose work Wellhausen founded his theory.

Wellhausen's forerunners were Karl David Ilgen (1763-1834), a German Protestant philologist (*Urkunden des Ersten Buchs Moses*, 1798); Wilhelm Martin Leberecht de Wette (1780-1849), (*Beitraege zur Einleitung in das Alte Testament*, 1806-1807); and Wilhelm Vatke (1806-1882) (*Die Geschichte des Heiligen Schriften des Alten Testaments*), who was highly influenced by Hegel. Vatke laid the foundation for Wellhausen's critique, and the latter admitted that he was indebted to Vatke "for the most and the best" of his own work. Ironically, Vatke, in his later days, retracted his conclusions, undermining many theories that Wellhausen later published!

7. See H. Wheeler Robinson, "The Contribution of Great Britain to Old Testament Study," *Expository Times* 41 (1929-1930): 46-50.

8. See J. M. Powis Smith, "The Contribution of the United States to Old Testament Scholarship," *Expository Times* 41 (1929-1930): 169-171.

9. See *Handkommentar zum Alten Testament*, 15 vols., ed. Wilhelm Nowack (Gottingen, 1892-1903); *Kurzer Handkommentar zum Alten Testament*, 20 vols., ed. Karl Marti (Freiburg, 1897-1904).

10. The following works summarize the literary criticism of the Wellhausen schools: John Edgar McFaydon, "The Present Position of Old Testament Criticism," in Arthur S. Peake, *The People and the Book*; "Modern Criticism," in H. Wheeler Robinson, ed., *Record and Revelation* (Oxford, 1938), pp. 74-109. For these and other important works in the field, see Herbert F. Hahn, *The Old Testament in Modern Research* (Philadelphia: Fortress Press, 1966).

11. One of the most important works following this line is Heinrich Holzinger's *Einleitung in den Hexateuch* (Freiburg, 1893). (According to some scholars, the J and E documents could also be traced through the Book of Joshua, so they spoke of the Hexateuch—six books). See Rudolf Smend's "JE in den geschichtlichen Buchern des Alten Testament," *Zeitschrift fuer die Alttestamentliche Wissenschaft* 49 (1921). Also see Rudolf Smend, *Die Erzaehlung des Hexateuch auf ihre Quellen des Genesis von neuem untersucht* (Giessen, 1916).

12. See J. H. Hertz, *The Pentateuch and the Haftarahs*, 2nd ed., (London: Soncino Press, 1962), p. 199.

13. Ibid.

14. *Alttestamentliche Studien* (Giessen, 1908, 1910, 1912).

15. See Hertz, *The Pentateuch and the Haftarahs*, p. 939. Kittel remarked on another occasion:

> Speaking for all branches of science we may say that a hypothesis which has stood for half a century has done its duty. Measured by this standard, Wellhausen's theory is as good as the best. However, there is increasing evidence that it has had its day and that those scholars, who from the first expressed serious doubts about it, were right. (Ibid., p. 941)

16. "*Die Aufgabe der Alttestamentlichen Forschung,*" *Zeitschrift fuer die Alttestamentliche Wissenschaft* 42 (1924): 8. See Hahn, *Old Testament in Modern Research*, p. 28.

17. See, for example, Adam C. Welch, *The Code of Deuteronomy: A New Theory of Its Origin* (London, 1924); see also Theodor Oestreicher, *Das Deuteronomische Grundgesetz* (Guthersloh, 1923) and Edward Robertson, *The Old Testament Problem* (Manchester, 1950).

18. A. Welch, *The Code of Deuteronomy*.

19. *Einleitung in das Alte Testament* (Tübingen, 1943).

20. On Holscher, see his *Komposition und Ursprung des Deuteronomi ums Zeitschrift fuer die Alttestamentliche Wissenschaft* 40 (1922).

21. See C. R. North, "Pentateuchal Criticism," in H. H. Rowley, ed., *The Old Testament and Modern Study* (Oxford, 1951).

22. S. R. Hirsch, *The Pentateuch, Translated and Explained*, tr. I. Levy (New York: Judaica Press, 1971).

23. *Die wichtigsten Instanzen gegen die Graf-Wellhausensche Hypothese* (vol. 1, 1903; vol. 2, 1916); *Das Buch Leviticus, uebersetzt und erklaert* (1905-1906); *Das Buch Deuteronomium, uebersetzt und erklaert* (1913-1922).

Most important are Hoffmann's refutations of the theory that the Priestly Code was a separate document composed after the Book of Deuteronomy and even after Ezekiel. Hoffmann showed that Leviticus was an earlier work than Deuteronomy and that Ezekiel was a derivative of it, rather than the other way around. Interesting is Hoffmann's belief referring to a statement in the Talmud (T. B. *Gittin* 60a) that Moshe composed the Torah in a series of scrolls that were written down after every revelation and later redacted into a single document.

24. In many unpublished papers. See A. Barth, *Dorenu Mul She'elat Ha-Netzach* (Jerusalem, 1952). In this book some important examples of Hoffmann's and Barth's arguments are presented.

25. *Dorot Harishonim,* 7 vols. (1897-1939, repr. 1967).

26. *The Documentary Hypothesis and the Composition of the Pentateuch,* trans. Israel Abrahams (English ed. [Jerusalem: Magnes Press, Hebrew University, 1961-1972]) or "The Theory òf Documents." Cassuto concludes (pp. 100-101):

> I have not shown that it was possible to solve the problems sin a different way from that of the documentary theory. I have shown that one must necessarily solve them otherwise and that it is impossible to solve them according to this system. I did not prove that the pillars are weak or that none of them is decisive. I have proved that they are not pillars at all, that they are non-existent and imaginary. Hence, I have arrived at the conclusion that the complete negation of the theory of documents is justified.

Other books by Cassuto in this field are *La questione della genesi* (1934), his commentaries on the books of Genesis and Exodus, and many other important papers.

27. *Toledot Ha-Emunah Ha-Yisraelit* (1937); abridged version in English, *The Religion of Israel,* translated and condensed by M. Greenberg (Jerusalem: Magnes Press, Hebrew University, 1960).

28. William F. Albright, *From the Stone Age to Christianity* (Baltimore: Anchor, 1957), pp. 84, 118-119.

29. W. L. Baxter (1841-1937), a Scottish Bible scholar, wrote, "Witnesses are reliable when they testify in favor of the critics, but their veracity is promptly impeached if their testimony is on the other side" (*Sanctuary and Sacrifice* [1892]); quoted in J. H. Hertz, *The Pentateuch and the Haftarahs* (London: Soncino Press, 1962), p. 556.

30. On Delitzch, see *Babel und Bibel* (Leipzig, 1902). See also Hugo Winckler, *Geschichte Israels*, vol. 2 (Berlin, 1900).

31. See *History, Archeology and Christian Humanism* (Baltimore: Anchor, 1942).

32. See W. R. Smith, *Lectures on the Religion of the Semites* (Edinburgh, 1889).

33. *Voelkerpsychologie*, 2 vols. (Leipzig, 1909).

34. *Israel: Its Life and Culture* (London, 1926; repr., 1940).

35. See E. Hardy, *Zur Geschichte der vergleichenden Religion forschung*, Archiv fur Religionswissenschaft 4 (1901).

36. *Moses, Ein Beitrag zur Untersuchung ueber die Urspruenge der Israelitischen Religion* (Tübingen, 1907).

37. *Altorientalischer und Israelitischer Monotheismus* (Tübingen, 1906), p. I. For an interesting comparison, see Maimonides, *Mishneh Torah: Hilchot Avodah Zarah*, introduction.

38. For an overview of this debate, see Henry Biberfeld, *Universal Jewish History* (Jerusalem: Feldheim, 1948), appendix, pp. 129-156.

39. Herman Wouk remarks in his book *This is My God* (Glasgow: Williams Collins Sons and Co., 1973) p. 291:

"Literary analysis has been used for generations by obsessive men to prove that everybody but Shakespeare wrote Shakespeare. I believe literary analysis could be used to prove that I wrote both *David Copperfield* and *Farewell to Arms*. I wish it were sound!"

40. *Israelitisch-Juedische Religionsgeschichte und alttestament- liche Theologie*, Zeitschrift fuer die Alttestamentliche Wissenschaft 44 (1962): 1-12.

41. *Theologie des Alten Testaments*, 3 vols. (Leipzig, 1933-1939). See "Guide to Understanding the Bible," *Journal of Biblical Literature* 65 (1946): 205-207.

42. *The Relevance of the Bible* (London, 1942). See also his *Rediscovery of the Old Testament* (London, 1946); Frank Glen Lankard, *The Bible Speaks to Our Generation* (New York, 1941); and Wyatt A. Smart, *Still the Bible Speaks* (New York, 1948).

43. Erich Auerbach, *Mimesis* (Princeton, NJ: Princeton University Press, 1971).

44. *The Art of Biblical Literature* (London: George Allen and Unwin, 1981).

45. *Image, Music, Text* (London: Fontana, 1977).

46. *A Remembered Future* (Bloomington, IN: Indiana University Press, 1984).

47. *The Craft of Biblical Narrative* (Hebrew) (Jerusalem: Molad, 1962).

48. *The Poetics of Biblical Narrative* (Bloomington, IN: Indiana University Press, 1985).

49. *Narrative Art in the Bible* (Sheffield, U.K.: Almond Press, 1989).

50. Most enlightening is Spinoza's observation that some texts of the Torah, such as the ones in Genesis 12:6; 22:14, and Deuteronomy 1:2, must have been written many years after Moshe's death, since they reveal information that refers to latter days. Spinoza relies here on the famous Jewish commentator Ibn Ezra (1088-1167), who wrote that these verses were "mysteries" about "which the wise should be silent" (on Deuteronomy 1:2). The traditional understanding of Ibn Ezra, as also confirmed by the modern Jewish scholar Samuel David Luzzatto (ShaDaL) (1800-1865), is that these passages must be understood as prophetic and anticipating the future. Here, the differences between the traditional approach and the ones of criticism become apparent. The critics were obviously not prepared to accept the "prophetic" dimension as suggested by tradition and consequently concluded that these passages could not have been written by Moshe. In other words, it was not the problems themselves that caused these differences of opinion but the very *approach* to the text that created these controversies.

51. See chapter 7.

52. "Emunah U-Madda Be-Parashanut Ha-Mikra," *Deot*, *Cheker Ha-Mikra Be-Machshavah Ha-Yehudit Ha-Datit He-Chadashah*, 11 (1959):18-25, 12 (1960): 13-27. See also Zvi Kurzweil, *The Modern Impulse of Traditional Judaism* (New York, 1985), pp. 79-91.

See also the critical comments by Jacob Katz, Uriel Simon, Joseph Heinemann, Meir Weiss, Dr. Halperin, and Jacov Zeidman in *Deot* 13 (1961): 14-23.

53. See Ish Shalom, *Avraham Isaac Kook: Between Rationalism and Mysticism* (Hebrew) Tel Aviv: Am Oved, 1990), pp. 98-115. Also see Zvi Yaron, *The Philosophy of Rabbi Kook* (Jerusalem: Eliner Library, 1991), pp. 188-189.

54. See also Franz Rosenzweig, *On Jewish Learning*, ed. Nahum Glatzer (New York: Schocken, 1955).

55. See H. S. Nijberg, *Studien zum Hoseabuch: Zugleich ein Beitrag zur Kehrung des Problems der Alttestestamentlichen Textkritik*. (Uppsala: Uppsala Universitets, Arskrift, 1935). For an overview, see E. Nielsen, *Oral Tradition: A Modern Problem in the Old Testament Introduction, Studies in Biblical Theology* 11 (Chicago, 1954); C. Stuhlmueller, "The Influence of Oral Tradition upon Exegeses and the Senses of Scripture," *Catholic Biblical Quarterly* 20 (1958): 299-326; B. Gerhardsson, *Memory and Manuscript; Oral Tradition and Written Transmission in Rabbinic Judaism and Early Christianity*, Acta seminarii neo-testamentici upsaliensis 22 (Uppsala, 1961); by the same author, *Muendliche und Schriftliche Tradition der Prophetenbuecher*, Theologische Literaturzeitung 17 (1961), pp. 216-220; and Michael Fishbane, *Biblical Interpretation in Ancient Israel* (Oxford: Clarendon Press, 1985). Herbert Schneidau's *Sacred Discontent* (Berkeley, CA: University of California Press, 1977) argues that textual tensions and apparent inconsistencies function as ways through which the reader becomes involved in the text. See also the important observations by J. F. Molitor, *Philosophie der Geschichte oder ueber die Tradition*, vol. 1 (Frankfurt, 1857), in which the author stresses the fact that in ancient times, the relationship of the written word and the

spoken word was very different and much more involved than in modern times.

56. See the introduction on Hirsch's commentary on the Torah by Dayan Dr. I. Grunfeld in Samson Raphael Hirsch, *The Pentateuch, Translation and Commentary*, Genesis (New York: Judaica Press, 1971), pp. viii-xxx.

57. *Judaism, Human Values, and the Jewish State* (Cambridge, MA: Harvard University Press, 1992), pp. 11-12.

58. Rabbi Simeon said:

Alas for the man who regards the Torah as a book of mere tales and everyday matters! If that were so, even we could compose a Torah dealing with everyday affairs and of *even greater excellence*. Nay, even the princes of the world possess books of *greater worth* which we could use as a model for composing some such Torah. The Torah, however, contains it all, its words are supernal truth. (*Zohar* III:152a) (italics added)

59. "The Lonely Man of Faith," *Tradition* 7:2 (Summer 1965).

60. H. S. Nijberg, quoted in Walter Kaufmann, *Critique of Religion and Philosophy* (Princeton, NJ: Princeton University Press, 1958), p. 384.

61. Ibid., p. 385.

62. See the author's *The Infinite Chain* (Jerusalem: Targum-Feldheim Press, 1989), pp. 35-42.

63. See Nachmanides on Ecclesiastes (*Kitvei Ha-Ramban*).

64. For a short overview of these thirty-two exegetical rules, see Hermann L. Strack, *Introduction to the Talmud and Midrash* (New York: Atheneum, 1978), pp. 95-98.

65. Quoted by M. Kapustin in "Biblical Criticism, a Tradionalist View," in *Challenge, Torah Views on Science and Its Problems*, ed. C. Domb and A. Carmel (Jerusalem: Feldheim, 1976), pp. 426-427. See also Chaim Hirschensohn, *Malki baKodesh*,

vol. 2 (St. Louis, MO: Moinster Printing Co., 1921), pp. 215-250, who points to a talmudic passage (tractate *Sofrim* 6:3) that states that there were three Torah scrolls in the Temple court that contained slight textual misreadings and that the correct reading was determined on the principle of following the majority.

CHAPTER 11

1. For some of the observations in this article I am indebted to Jacob J. Petuchowski's *Understanding Jewish Prayer* (New York: Ktav, 1972).

2. T. B. *Shabbat* 115b.

3. T. B. *Berachot* 33b.

4. *Yoma* 5:2.

References

Abravanel, Don Yitzchak. *Perush al Ha-Torah*. 15th cent.

Albright, William F. *From the Stone Age to Christianity*. Baltimore: Anchor, 1957.

——. *History, Archeology and Christian Humanism*. Baltimore: Anchor, 1942.

Alter, Robert. *The Art of Biblical Literature*. London: George Allen and Unwin, 1981.

Arama, Yitzchak. *Akeidat Yitzchak, Perush al Ha-Torah*. 15th cent.

Auerbach, Erich. *Mimesis*. Princeton, NJ: Princeton University Press, 1971.

Azulai, Avraham. *Chesed Le-Avraham*. Sulzbach, 1685.

Barth, Aharon. *Dorenu Mul She'elat Ha-Netzach (The Modern Jew Faces the Eternal Problems)*. Jerusalem: Ha-Hisdradut Ha-Tzionit Ha-Olamit, Ha-Machlakah Le-Chinuch U-le-Tarbut Torani im Ba-Golah, 1952.

Barthes, Roland. *Image, Music, Text*. London: Fontana, 1977.

Baxter, W. L. *Sanctuary and Sacrifice*. Scotland, 1892.

Beaulieu, A. Leroy. *Israel among the Nations*. 1893.

Berdyaev, Nicholas. *The Meaning of History*. 1933.

Biberfeld, Henry. *Universal Jewish History*. Jerusalem: Feldheim, 1948.

Bloch, E. *Naturrecht und Menschliche Wuerde*. Frankfurt am Main, 1961.

Breuer, Mordechai. *Emunah U-Madda Be-Parashanut Ha-Mikra, De'ot. Cheker Ha-Mikra Be-Machashavah Ha-Yehudit Ha-Datit He-Chadash.* Vols. 11, 12. Jerusalem, 1959, 1960.

Cassuto, Umberto. *The Documentary Hypothesis and the Composition of the Pentateuch.* Trans. Israel Abrahams. Jerusalem: Magnes Press, Hebrew University, 1961–1972.

——. *A Commentary on the Book of Genesis.* Part 1: From Adam to Noah. Trans. Israel Abrahams. Jerusalem: Magnes Press, Hebrew University, 1972, 1978.

——. *A Commentary on the Book of Exodus.* Trans. Israel Abrahams. Jerusalem: Magnes Press, Hebrew University, 1967, 1974, 1983.

Chajes, Zvi Hirsch. *Kol Sifrei Maharitz Chayot.* Jerusalem: Mosad HaRav Kook, 1958.

Deutcher, Isaac. *The non-Jewish Jew and other Essays.* New York: Oxford University Press, 1968.

Eerdmans, B. D. *Alttestamentliche Studien.* Giessen, 1908, 1910, 1912.

Efrati, B. *Hazon Ha-Geulah Be-Mishnat Ha-Rav Kook.* Jerusalem: Mosad HaRav Kook, 1956.

Eissfeldt, Otto. *Einleitung in das Alttestestament.* Tübingen, 1943.

——. *Israelitisch-Juedische Religiongeschichte und Alttestamentliche Theologie. Zeitschrift fuer die Alttestamentliche Wissenschaft,* 1962.

Eliashov, Shlomo. *Sefer Le-Shem She-Vo Ve-Achlama.* Jerusalem, repr. 1973.

Fisch, Harold. *A Remembered Future.* Bloomington, IN: Indiana University Press, 1984.

Fischbane, Michael. *Biblical Interpretation in Ancient Israel.* Oxford: Clarendon, 1977.

Frazer, James G. *The Golden Bough: A Study in Magic and Religion.* London, 1890.

Fromm, Erich. *To Have or to Be?* New York: HarperCollins, 1976.

Gerhardsson, B. *Memory and Manuscript, Oral Tradition and Written Transmission in Rabbinic Judaism and Early Christian-*

ity. Acta seminarii neo-testamentici upsaliensis. Uppsala, 1961.

———. *Muendliche und Schriftliche Tradition der Prophetenbuecher.* Theologische Literaturzeitung 17, 1961.

Gershom, Levi ben. *Perush al Bereshit.* 14th cent.

Gikatila, Ibn Joseph. *Sha'arei Orah.* Offenbach, 1715.

Gordis, Robert. *Judaic Ethics for a Lawless World.* New York: Jewish Theological Seminary of America, 1986.

Grotius, Hugo. *De Juri Belli ad Pacis.* Holland, 17th cent.

Grunfeld, I. *The Sabbath, A Guide to Its Understanding and Observance.* New York: Feldheim, 1959.

Halevi, Jehuda. *Kuzari.* Trans. Avraham Davis. Metsuda, NY: Rabbi Jacob Joseph School Press, 1979.

Halevi, Yitzchak Isaac. *Dorot Ha-Rishonim.* Jerusalem, 1897-1939. Repr. 1967.

Hardy, E. *Zur Geschichte der vergleichenden Religionforschung.* Archiv fur Religionwissenschaft 4, 1901.

Hertz, Joseph Herman. *A Book of Jewish Thoughts.* London: Oxford University Press, 1966.

———. *The Pentateuch and the Haftarahs.* London: Soncino Press, 1962.

Heschel, Avraham Yehoshua. *God in Search of Man.* New York: Farrar, Straus and Giroux, 1955.

Hick, John. *Philosophy of Religion.* Englewood Cliffs, NJ: Prentice-Hall, 1983.

Hirsch, Samson Raphael. *The Nineteen Letters on Judaism.* Adapted by Jacob Breuer, translated by Dr. Bernard Drachman. New York: Feldheim Publishers, 1969.

———. *The Pentateuch, Translated and Explained.* Trans. Isaac Levy. New York: Judaica Press, 1971.

Hirschensohn, Chaim. *Malki Ba-Kodesh.* St. Louis, MO: Moinster Printing Co., 1921.

Hoffmann, David. *Das Buch Deuteronomium, uebersetzt und erklaert.* 1913-1922.

———. *Das Buch Leviticus, uebersetzt und erklaert.* 1905-1906.

——. *Die wichtigsten Instanzen gegen die Graf-Wellhausensche Hypothese*, 1903, 1916.

Holscher, Gustav. *Komposition und Ursprung des Deuteronomi ums Zeitschrift fur die Alttestamentliche Wissenschaft* 40. 1922.

Holzinger, Heinrich. *Einleitung in den Hextateuch*. Freiburg, 1893.

Ibn Ezra. *Perush al Ha-Torah*, 11-12th cent.

Ilgen, Karl David. *Urkunden des Ersten Buchs Moses*, 1789.

Isaac the Blind. *Commentary on Midrash Konen*, Beth Midrash. Jellineck, 1853.

James, William. *Principles of Psychology*. New York: Macmillan and Co., 1898.

Jung, Carl Gustav. *Essays on Contemporary Events*. London: Kegan Paul, 1936.

Kant, Immanuel. *Groundwork of the Metaphysics of Morals*. Translated and explained by H. J. Paton in *The Moral Law*. London: Hutchinson, 1948.

Kapustin, M. "*Biblical Criticism, a Traditionalist View*." In *Challenge, Torah Views on Science and Its Problems*. Ed. C. Domb and A. Carmel. Jerusalem: Feldheim, 1976.

Kaufman, Yechezkel. *Toledot Ha-Emunah Ha-Yisraelit*. Jerusalem: Magnes Press, Hebrew University, 1960. Jerusalem, 1937. Translated and condensed by M. Greenberg. Jerusalem, 1960.

Kaufmann, Walter. *Critique of Religion and Philosophy*. Princeton, NJ: Princeton University Press, 1979.

Kimchi, David. *Perush al HaTorah*. 13th cent.

Kitov, Eliyahu. *The Book of Our Heritage*. Jerusalem: Feldheim, 1978.

Lankard, Frank Glen. *The Bible Speaks to Our Generation*. New York, 1941.

Leibowitz, Nechama. *Studies in Shemoth*. Jerusalem: World Zionest Organization Department for Torah Education and Culture, 1972.

Leibowitz, Yeshayahu. *Judaism, Human Values and the Jewish State*. Cambridge, MA: Harvard University Press, 1992.

Lopes Cardozo, Nathan T. *The Infinite Chain*. New York: Targum Press, 1989.

Luzzatto, Samuel David. *Perush al Ha-Torah*. 19th cent.

Maimonides, Moses. *Guide of the Perplexed*. Translated with an introduction and notes by Shlomo Pines. Chicago: University of Chicago Press, 1963.

——. *Mishneh Torah*. Jerusalem, 11th cent.

——. *Perush al Ha-Mishnah*. Jerusalem, 11th cent.

——. *Shemonah Perakim*. Jerusalem, 11th cent.

Malbim, Meir Levush. *Perush al Ha-Torah*. Jerusalem, 19th cent.

Martin, Karl, ed. *Kurzer Handkommentar zum Alten Testament*. Freiburg, 1879-1904.

Mayer, Carl. "Religious and Political Aspects of Anti-Judaism." In *Jews in a Gentile World*. Ed. Graebner and Britt. New York: Macmillan, 1942.

Molitor, J. F. *Philosophie der geschichte oder ueber die Tradition*. Frankfurt, 1857.

Nachmanides, Moses. *Perush al Ha-Torah*. Jerusalem, 12th cent.

——. *Perush al Kohelet. Kitvei Ha-Ramban*. Ed. Chaim Dov Chavel. Jerusalem: Mosad HaRav Kook, 1963.

Nicoll, Maurice. *Living Time*. London, 1952.

Nielsen, E. *Oral Tradition: A Modern Problem in the Old Testament Introduction*. Studies in Biblical Theology. Chicago, 1954.

Nijberg, H. S. *Studien zum Hoseabuch: Zugleich ein Beitrag zur Kehrung des Problems der Alttestamentlichen Textkritik*. Uppsala: Uppsala Universitets, 1935.

Novack, Wilhelm, ed. *Handkommentar zum Alten Testament*. Gottingen, 1892-1903.

Novak, David. *The Image of the Non-Jew in Judaism*. Lewiston, NY: Edwin Mellen Press, 1984.

Oestreicher, Theodor. *Das Deuteronomische Grundgesetz*. Guthersloh, 1923.

Otto, Rudolf. *Das Heilige*. Breslau, 1917.

Pascal, Blaise. *Pensees*. 17th cent.

Peake, Arthur S. *The People and the Book, Modern Criticism*. Oxford, 1925.

Pedersen, Johannes. *Israel, Its Life and Culture*. London, 1926; repr., 1940.

Petuchowski, Jacov. *Spontaneity and Tradition in Understanding Jewish Prayer.* New York: Ktav, 1972.

Powes Smith, J. M. "The Contribution of the United States to Old Testament Scholarship." *Expository Times* 41 (1929-1930).

Rashi. *Perush al Ha-Torah.* 11th cent.

Recanati, Menachem. *Perush al Ha-Torah.* 14th cent.

——. *Ta'amei Ha-Mitzvot.* Basel, 1581.

Robertson, Edward. *The Old Testament Problem.* Manchester, 1950.

Robinson, H. Wheeler. "The Contribution of Great Britain to Old Testament Study." *Expository Times* 41 (1929-1930).

——. *Record and Revelation.* Oxford, 1938.

Rosenzweig, Franz. *On Jewish Learning.* Ed. Nahum Glatzer. New York: Shocken, 1955.

Rowley, H. H. *The Rediscovery of the Old Testament.* London, 1946.

——. *The Relevance of the Bible.* London, 1942.

Scheidau, Herbert. *Sacred Discontent.* Berkeley: University of California Press, 1977.

Sefer Yetzirah. Republished by Mordechai Attiya. Jerusalem, 1972.

Selden, John. *De Jure Naturale et gentium Juxta Disciplinam Ebraerum.* 1665.

Sforno, Ovadia. *Perush al Ha-Torah.* 15th cent.

Shalom, Ish. *Avraham Isaac Kook: Between Rationalism and Mysticism.* Tel Aviv: Am Oved, 1990.

Shimon bar Efrat. *Narrative Art in the Bible.* Sheffield: Almond Press, 1959.

Shumacher, E. F. *A Guide for the Perplexed.* New York: Harper Colophon Books, 1977.

Simcha Zissel of Kelm. *Chochmah U-Mussar.* 20th cent.

Smart, Wyatt A. *Still the Bible Speaks.* New York, 1948.

Smend, Rudolf. *Die Erzaehlung des Hexateuch auf ihre Quellen des Genesis von neuem untersucht.* Giessen, 1916.

Smith, W. R. *Lectures on Religion of the Semites.* Edinburgh, 1889.

Soloveitchik, Joseph Ber. "The Lonely Man of Faith." *Tradition* 7:2 (1965).

Spiegel, Simon. *Hebrew Reborn.* 1930.

Spinoza, Benedictus de. *A Theologico-Political Treatise*. Trans. R. H. M. Elwes. New York: Dover, 1951.

Sternberg, Meir. *The Poetics of Biblical Narrative*. Bloomington, IN: Indiana University Press, 1985.

Strack, L. *Introduction to the Talmud and Midrash*. New York: Atheneum, 1978.

Stulmueller, C. "The Influence of Oral Tradition upon Exegeses and the Senses of Scripture." *Catholic Biblical Quarterly* 20 (1958).

Toynbee, Arnold. *Studies of History*. 1961.

Tyrrel, G. N. M. *Grades of Significance*. London, 1930.

Vital, Chaim. *Sha'arei Ma'amrei Razal*. 1890.

Volozhin, Chaim. *Nefesh Ha-Chaim*. 19th cent.

Weinberg, Yechiel Jacov. *Sridei Esh*. Vol. 2. Jerusalem: Mosad HaRav Kook, 1966.

Weiss, Meir. *The Craft of Biblical Narrative*. Jerusalem: Molad, 1962.

Welch, Adam C. *The Code of Deuteronomy, a New Theory of Its Origin*. London, 1924.

Wellhausen, Julius. *Prolegomena to the History of Israel*. Edinburgh: A. and C. Black, 1885.

Wette de, Martin Leberecht. *Beitraege zur Einleitung in das Alte Testaments*. Halle, 1806-1807.

Winckler, Hugo. *Geschichte Israels*. Berlin, 1900.

Wouk, Herman. *This Is My God*. Glasgow: William Collins Sons and Co., 1973.

Wundt, Wilhelm. *Voelkerpsychologie*. Leipzig, 1909.

Yaron, Zvi. *The Philosophy of Rav Kook*. Jerusalem: Eliner Library, 1991.

Zangwill, Israel. *Speeches, Articles and Letters*. London, 1937.

Zunz, Leopold. *Synagogale Poesie des Mittelalters*, 1836.

Index

ABOUT THE AUTHOR

Nathan T. Lopes Cardozo, originally from Amsterdam, Holland, is well known throughout America, Canada, South Africa, and Europe for his lectures on Jewish philosophy. He received rabbinic ordination from Gateshead Talmudic College in England and holds a Ph.D. from Columbia Pacific University. He lectures at Ohr Somayach College for Jewish Studies and at Michlala-Jerusalem College for Women in Jerusalem, where he lives with his wife, children, and grandchildren. He is the author of *The Infinite Chain*, *Torah Mesora and Man*, and *The Torah as God's Mind*, as well as many articles on Jewish thought. He frequently lectures at outreach programs, synagogues, and university campuses in Israel and in English-speaking countries.